The American Bridge to
the Israel Commonwealth

Books by Bernard A. Rosenblatt

SOCIAL ZIONISM
FEDERATED PALESTINE AND THE JEWISH COMMONWEALTH
THE AMERICAN BRIDGE TO THE ISRAEL COMMONWEALTH

The American Bridge to
the Israel Commonwealth

By BERNARD A. ROSENBLATT

FARRAR, STRAUS AND CUDAHY

New York

Dedicated to the memory of the great American jurist
LOUIS D. BRANDEIS
who personified the social ideals of American Zionism

Foreword

More than two-thirds of all Jews in the world today live in the United States and Israel. With Roumanian Jewry on the march and with the possibility of a mass migration from other countries of Eastern Europe now definitely on the horizon, it is to be assumed that Israel and the United States between them will soon account for the overwhelming majority of the Jewish people everywhere.

A bridge between the Jewish community of America and the state of Israel has long been a primary necessity. With the growing interrelations of the two countries, this bridge of understanding, of exchange of ideas and of knowhow, has become a matter of vital importance to the Jewish state as well as an indispensable condition for the growth and development of American Jewry.

To this end Judge Bernard A. Rosenblatt makes a definite contribution in his clearly thought out and closely knit work. Having spent many years of his life in what was once Palestine and is today Israel in applying American ideas to the economy of the ancient land, Judge Rosenblatt is particularly qualified to point to the beneficent influence of American thought and practice when brought to bear on the life and development of the Jewish Homeland.

It is no accident that Judge Rosenblatt stresses the social aspects of the Jewish National Fund, notably its land tenure policy, as one of the cornerstones of Social Zionism which he would like to see established in Israel. As one of the chief architects with Justice Brandeis, of the famous Pittsburgh Platform, which for a generation has inspired the pioneers and builders of Zion, Judge Rosenblatt could not but discern in the Jewish National Fund the classic instrument of land reform which is everywhere the basis of all social advance. Noteworthy in this connection is President Truman's characterization of the Jewish National Fund as "America's Point Four projected fifty years earlier."

Judge Rosenblatt's ideas about other reforms in Israel, which would combine the best features of non-Marxian socialism and American free enterprise in the reconstruction of Israel's economy, deserve to be read and pondered by all true friends of the Jewish Homeland.

Dr. Harris J. Levine,
President, Jewish National
Fund of America

Contents

Preface

Throughout history, justice has been the keynote of the Hebraic character—and the striving for social justice is the major theme in the message of the Hebrew prophets. It is, therefore, only reasonable to assume that the new state of Israel will continue the golden thread of Jewish history in the great struggle for justice among men. Indeed, the founder of modern Zionism, after writing the *Judenstaat*, closed his career with *Altneuland*, wherein he continued the prophecy of a Jewish state as a model community, rendering individual justice to the "stranger within the gates" and social justice among all classes of the community.

It was this social aspect of Zionism that made a special appeal, in the early days, to American Jews, when the first College Zionist Society was organized at Columbia University, in 1905, and a similar one was established almost simultaneously at Harvard University. Two years later, in the enthusiasm of his youth, the writer of this book won a coveted oratorical prize on the subject of "Palestine, the Future Hebrew State," from which the following quotation may serve as a challenge and a promise:

"In the olden days, when Egypt, Assyria and Babylon were the triumphant but merciless military despotisms, the first Hebrew state gave to the world the concept of monotheism and the fundamental principles of morality, embellished by the thoughts of prophets and the rhetoric of poets. A few centuries later, when Rome was completing her conquest of the World, the second Hebrew state—the state built by the heroism of the Maccabees—gave Christianity to the world, to civilize Europe and prepare it for further advances. Today, we are entering the social era of the world's history. Will the Jew prove true to his old self and present to the world an example of a moral-social community—a true commonwealth—resting on the foundation of social justice?"

Within a decade, the phrase "social Zionism" was used time and again to describe the striving for a social commonwealth, and it was emphasized in a book of essays titled *Social Zionism*.

Since the establishment of the state of Israel, this struggle for a just social system is the manifest destiny of the new Israel commonwealth. Mistakes have been made in this difficult period in the early history of the revived state of Israel but, fortunately, such mistakes can be remedied in the light of American experience. A generation ago, when Europeans generally, and leaders of world Zionism in particular, were as dubious about American interference in social ideals as in cultural ideology, such a suggestion would hardly have received serious consideration. Today, however, American "knowhow" is welcomed and accorded respectful attention everywhere.

In this connection, I recall a memorable incident in the spring of 1921, while I was presiding at a meeting on the East Side of New York at the Hebrew Trade School. Dr. Chaim Weizmann was the chief speaker. I was then serving as a Justice in the New York City Magistrate Court and had prevailed on the Mayor to offer the freedom of the City of New York to Dr. Chaim Weizmann and his fellow visitor from abroad, Professor Albert Einstein. This was the first time that any Jew was so honored.

Dr. Weizmann had designated me as his personal representative in an effort to make peace in the factional struggle within the American Zionist movement, then under the presidency of Judge Julian W. Mack, who was strongly supported by the great leader of American Zionism, Justice Louis D. Brandeis. In my youthful innocence, I was convinced that a common ground might be found to avoid an open conflict at the forthcoming Zionist convention in Cleveland, where the Brandeis-Mack forces were later defeated. To my surprise and astonishment, as I introduced Dr. Weizmann to the meeting, he began his address with the startling phrase: "There is no bridge between Pinsk and Washington."

I then realized the gap that separated the principles of the great austere Justice in Washington from the equally great son of East European Jewry who was to become the first President of Israel. But when I later expostulated with Dr. Weizmann for that particular phrase, he confessed that he could not resist the temptation to use it as a contrast between East European Jewry and the West. I am now more than ever convinced that such a bridge, even longer and stronger, stretching all the way from Washington and New York to Tel Aviv, Haifa and Jerusalem, must be built. This book is an effort to help build such a bridge.

The state of Israel today represents the only effective challenge to communism that is not based on military force. The latter may sometimes be necessary as a matter of self-defense, but force alone may be self-defeating even when victorious, for military conquest will seldom change the minds of men. Communism must be met on the spiritual plane—in a free exchange of ideas and the liberty of action which makes possible the development of economic theories and practices in competition with the all-devouring Marxian dialectics. Nowhere else— neither in democratic England nor in freedom-loving America—is the clash of social ideals and economic theories so welcome as in Israel. Under the free democratic system of that state the Communist Party, operating without any restrictions, has been able to enlist barely 2 per cent of a population that has faced almost insuperable economic difficulties in this critical period since its Declaration of Independence in May, 1948. The masses in that little country naturally prefer the voluntary socialism of their cooperative farm settlements (the Kvutzah system) to the dictates of a coercive communist state, while all are still free to compete in the wider field of the industrial life of the country.

Where there is complete freedom of press and speech, and where communism is not proscribed politically or socially, it has to meet the challenge of a freedom-loving democracy that traces its traditions all the way from the prophets of the Old Testament. In such an atmosphere of freedom, communism, with its concept of statism, cannot thrive, even when there are no restrictions to its development.

Indeed, we must always remember that the real and fundamental objection to communism is not so much its Marxian theory (which conceivably might be able to defeat capitalism in an ideological struggle), but rather its subordination of individual liberty to the demands of an all-devouring state. It is precisely here where Israel, with its biblical traditions of the worth of the individual and the principles of social justice, cannot possibly accept the overriding theory of a communist state. This is best illustrated in the field of economics, where the strong labor unions in Israel have become virtually capital-labor trusts, combining with individual entrepreneurs, on the one hand, and, on the other, often assuming partial state activities.

It is precisely, too, in the latter area that the state of Israel may profit from American experience and, more particularly, in the field of anti-trust legislation and the regulation of monopolies.

Some years ago many Zionists, particularly in America, were disturbed by a debate in the Knesset, the Israel Parliament, over economic restrictions which seemed to many of us the outgrowth of some dogmas of the Labor Party as the dominant power in the state. As a good friend and admirer of the Prime Minister, David Ben-Gurion, I complained to him about what I regarded as needless restrictions, which necessarily prevented the flow of American capital into the state of Israel. I wrote as follows:

"Has it never occurred to you that the reason for the failure to receive the maximum support from American Jewry, to which you are entitled, may be due, at least in a large measure, to the failure of your administration to understand the principles upon which American democracy operates in the economic field, and to which American Jews are irrevocably committed? We have no quarrel with your socialist purpose. I was one of the framers of the Pittsburgh Platform, under the inspired leadership of Justice Louis D. Brandeis, and I dare say that this pronouncement of American Zionism of a generation ago still stands as a model of social justice toward which Israel may well strive. There is a real difference of opinion, however, about the needless restrictions on economic life with its permits and licenses, so reminiscent of a 'ukase' of some ancient Czar. These are not even submitted to the Knesset and did not properly form an integral part of socialist doctrine (as expressed in the nationalization of the 'tools of production'), but stem rather from a philosophy of centralization springing from Eastern and Central Europe which had wrecked the economics of half the world. But for these useless and unnecessary restrictions, you would have had a flow of hundreds of millions of investing dollars from American Jews, *together with the sons of such investors to protect their money.*"

I received a reply which was on the whole reassuring, as evidenced by the following quotation:

"As for American Jewry (and this of course includes the Zionists in America) I believe it rendered its assistance and will continue to do so willingly and with a warm Jewish heart. I cannot say anything on the 'maximum support' as expressed by you in your letter, but I believe that American Jewry has given and will continue to give great help and support.

"I do not know whether you are right in saying that our administration has failed to understand 'the principles upon which American democracy operates in the economic field and to which American Jews are irrevocably committed' and I doubt whether there is such an 'irrevocable commitment.' I do know, however, that there is a great difference between the principles of Hoover and Coolidge and those of Roosevelt and Truman and anyway I do not believe that even America has frozen principles which stand from the time of the establishment of the American Republic to this day. Both in the political and economic fields, many things have changed and with every change there are staunch supporters of the old ways who disagree and fight any deviation from 'irrevocable principles.' In spite of this, however, the earth does revolve and things do change.

"There may be differences of opinions as to whether permits are needed but I regret that you found it necessary to compare the controls imposed in Israel with the 'ukase' of the Russian Czar. Our democracy is allowed to go her way; you are quite right in thinking that the restrictions and controls prevalent here are not an integral part of the socialist doctrine and did not stem from socialist motives, just as the control and rationing in the States during the war were not the result of socialist doctrine. These controls are dictated by our particular conditions which have no parallel in any other country—the result of unequaled mass immigration.

"Permit me further to remark that I was never a Marxist —although Marxism is permissible in our midst and I find no shame in this, but personally I do not belong to this school of thought.

"I know we have a great deal to learn from America. But there is a fundamental difference between learning and imitating. I am prepared to learn endlessly the American technical knowhow. The rest I will examine according to its merits. If it suits us—I will accept it; if it doesn't —I will not. The fact alone that this is the way it is done in America does not bind me at all.

"On one point I agree with you and that is that our economic problem is grave and calls for great and concentrated efforts. I believe we will solve this problem and overcome the difficulties. We need time. The United States too were in need of foreign loans for about one hundred and fifty years. I am sure that we shall attain economic independence in a much shorter time and will not require one-tenth of the time which the great and rich America required. We will do this our own way—

1. By encouraging private enterprise and private capital.
2. By ensuring, as far as we can, the minimum necessities for everybody.
3. By expanding industry, enhancing productivity and increasing exports."

This blunt statement by the dynamic leader of the state of Israel points the way for cooperation between the great democracy of the West and the little outpost of freedom and democracy in the Holy Land. Nor is the relationship merely that of donor and recipient, even when Jewish funds flow from the West to the East. It is because I am convinced that we have much to learn from the institutions already firmly established in the state of Israel that the spiritual bridge between America and the Holy Land must be built.

No one can deny that considerable progress has already been made by the state of Israel in the age-long struggle for social justice. It is our fond hope that from the lessons in the hard school of American experience, such a message may indeed prove a "light unto the nations." Mankind must find a road, however rough and rocky, that shall avoid, on the one hand, the Scylla of slavery in a communist state, and the Charybdis of a devouring fascism on the other. Perhaps for a third time, the still, small voice, coming from the hills of Galilee and the valley of the Sharon up to the mountains of Judea, may once again sound the true word which may yet bring peace with justice in an Atomic Age.

Bernard A. Rosenblatt

New York City
November, 1958

CHAPTER ONE

Israel's Relation
to World Jewry

Many prominent Jews, particularly in Western Europe and America, formerly refused to accept the philosophy of Zionism because of their insistence that Judaism was merely a religion—that they were adherents of a world-wide faith which did not have any political connotation. In America this was emphasized by the general character of the people as a whole and the underlying principles of the Constitution of the United States. The American nation, with racial roots in most of the European countries, never made a fetish of its Aryanism or racial purity, although for the greater part of its history Anglo-Saxon blood predominated. Furthermore, starting its national life in 1776, when all Christian sects, from Quakers to Catholics, were represented (and even a sprinkling of Jews) in the thirteen original states, Americans have always taken to heart the injunction of the great Jefferson that free exercise of religion, as a natural right is a sacred trust later safeguarded in the Bill of Rights by the federal government as a national heritage.

It was, therefore, perfectly logical for many American

Jews, with only a slight knowledge of the historical background of Judaism, to accept the simple thesis that they were "Jews by religion only," but basically Americans, like the adherents of every other faith. Of course, that does not dispose of the proposition that Negroes, whether Catholic or Protestant, are likewise Americans, and all good American Catholics still maintain the spiritual connection with the Vatican, which exists as an independent sovereign state. Like Negroes who may take pride in the progress of Liberia and Irish Catholics who are proud of the Irish Republic and like all American Catholics, who look to the Pope as their spiritual head, so there is every reason to expect that Americans of Jewish faith should look with favor upon the role which the state of Israel may play in the annals of mankind. Now that Israel is a state *de facto* and *de jure*, there is little likelihood of anyone raising the false issue of double allegiance. For it is the accepted rule that in any real crisis, everyAmerican—Jew and Gentile alike—naturally responds by putting America first.

There never was any excuse for the implied assumption that no Jewish community *anywhere* could ever develop into a nation. History has no record of any debate among the English Puritans who boarded the *Mayflower,* or the Quakers under William Penn who followed their example sixty years later, as to whether their own group of immigrants constituted a nation, a race, or merely a religious community. Presumably, the mere fact of discrimination and persecution was sufficient to impel these wanderers to establish thriving commonwealths across the Atlantic— even as the Czarist persecution over sixty years ago in the generation before World War I was responsible for the first Jewish colonization efforts in Palestine, and the Nazi reign of terror later resulted in a large-scale immigration that made possible the evolution of the state of Israel.

The Pilgrim fathers migrated first to Holland, where full religious freedom was accorded them, about the same time as the parents of Spinoza breathed the free air of Amsterdam as refugees from intolerant Spain. Yet the Puritan ancestors of New England remained dissatisfied in peaceful Holland because, as our school history books so quaintly tell us, "they did not want their children to lose their English ways," including, of course, the English language. So they risked the unknown dangers of an ocean voyage, more than three centuries ago, and paid a fearful toll in Indian warfare in order to establish a New England overseas. Spinoza's compatriots were not so far-sighted, perhaps because they had no Hebrew language or strong traditions to safeguard, but only "Spanish ways" to lose, and so their descendants later paid a terrible price in Nazi concentration camps and in Polish extermination centers.

This plain historic fact stares us in the face: Whenever any group is subject to such severe discrimination that their lives are put in jeopardy, they do not stop to philosophize about their plight, but move onward to a territory where they may erect a state or commonwealth to safeguard their progeny. The French Huguenots failed to erect a state in the New World only because the Spanish Inquisition destroyed their colonies in Florida, while the French Jesuits thwarted their colonization efforts in Canada. But the Mormons, no different in language or race from other Americans, after facing persecution in the East, trekked across the great American desert to establish

21

their "holy land" in the state of Utah, with its center at Salt Lake City. Since there is now a firmly established state of Israel, it may well serve as a house of refuge for a "saving remnant" of a couple of million Jews from some intolerant countries in Christian Europe, as well as from Moslem Africa and Asia. Shall we be deflected from such a course by a mere religious theory of negation, discredited by history itself, whether in the foundation of Puritan New England, Quaker Pennsylvania, Mormon Utah, or Catholic Quebec?

The relation of American Jews to the state of Israel may closely parallel the relation of American Catholics to the Papal State and the Vatican. Of course, there can never be any question of double allegiance. The state of Israel will permit only its citizens (Jews and Arabs alike and whatever be their religious beliefs or non-beliefs) to vote and determine its internal and external policies. Yet the spiritual connection between the largest Jewish community (for America now holds nearly one-half of the Jews of the world) and the infant state of Israel where Jews constitute a large majority of the population, will be necessarily close, based upon the common religion, similar traditions and a heritage of two thousand years of history.

The old-time Zionists in America, as elsewhere, will necessarily have to readjust their time-worn propaganda based upon nation and nationality. In the state of Israel the Jews constitute a nation, as in America they form a great religious community, with Judaism as the firm basis of their faith. This may not suit the few iconoclasts who are accustomed to assert so blatantly that they are Jews, yet have no religion. For them, a secure place may be found in the state of Israel, together with a great majority who profess Judaism. In America, however, which daily salutes the flag as "one nation indivisible," there is no room for conflicting nations.

Nor should we have much sympathy for those refined philosophies that seek to establish a new principle based upon "Jewish civilization" or "Jewish culture." Why should anyone, particularly Jewish ministers of religion (for some Rabbis are its chief exponents), seek to hide their Judaism under the cloak of "civilization" or "culture"? Judaism was never a mere Sabbath observance creed. It was always a *way of life*. And if that means "Jewish civilization" is it not better to call it by the old name of Judaism, which every American can understand and respect, as a religion guaranteed under the Constitution? Why attempt to build a new structure and denominate it "culture," when the living waters of Judaism are broad and deep enough to cover all the shades of Jewish religious beliefs and practices—a term which every American, Jew and Gentile alike, can fully appreciate?

Shall we engage in a fruitless battle over terminology, like the Blues and Greens in an ancient amphitheatre, when all the time America is ready and willing to accept the principle of religious demarcation, but not that of nation or nationality? No true American will ever question the religious content of any creed so long as the practices of its adherents do not constitute grave misdemeanors nor violate the moral code. Accordingly, it remains for us only to point out the simple fact that the "Restoration of Zion" is part and parcel of our ancient Judaism—and we need only offer our prayerbooks and the words of the prophets of Israel as conclusive evidence that the rebuilding of Jerusalem and the re-establishment of the state of Israel is enjoined upon us as a religious duty. Most American Jews will probably never behold the Land of Promise with earthly eyes, but they may solace themselves with the words of the great teacher Moses, who did not cross the Jordan, but who left the heritage of "Israel restored" as part of the Jewish creed and faith.

It may, indeed, seem strange that we so often stumble over terms and definitions. Many citizens of the British Isles, the Scots, and even the Welsh, regard themselves as separate nations within the British Commonwealth. An Englishman may boast with dry humor that during the Peace Conference at the conclusion of World War I, Great Britain was represented by five delegates, and not a single one a member of the English nation. There was Lloyd George, the Welshman; Balfour, the Scotsman; Smuts, the South African Boer; General Wilson, an Irishman; and finally, Milner, who was half English, but who was born in Germany. Yet in America, if Justice Felix Frankfurter, Ralph Bunche, representative of the United Nations, and our present Secretary of State were to draw up a final peace treaty for settlement of the problems in the Near East, all of them would simply be classified as members of the American nation, despite their racial affiliations.

In short, the Jews in the state of Israel constitute a nation of Israelis. The bond between them and their American brethren is one of ancient blood and, what is far more important for the future, the "historic connection" from Moses to modern days, the common religion known and recognized as Judaism. It adds nothing to describe this faith as a culture or civilization, but simply invites misrepresentation on the part of some critics who rightly insist upon the indivisibility of the American nation.

The Jews of Israel, too, may have to readjust their views to some extent. I recall a visit many years ago to a Hebrew school in Tiberias, on the shores of the Lake of Galilee, where pupils in the geography class were reciting lessons about the various countries of Europe; almost invariably, after indicating the industries, the products and the character of the population and statistics of the country, there was a refrain "Roumania has 800,000 Jews" or "Bulgaria has 50,000 Jews," etc., as if they constituted independent flora and fauna in each country. But it was only to the American visitor that this seemed odd or surprising. Those from Eastern Europe accepted it as an essential fact, and this perhaps illustrates the whole problem. In Eastern and Central Europe the Jews were never merely a religious group, but a distinct nation—as exemplified by the history of the Austro-Hungarian Empire, which consisted of a medley of nationalities.

Indeed, the whole Mediterranean basin is often regarded as the national home of the Jewish people. I recall an interesting dinner party years ago on an island in the Nile, where the host gave Cairo as his birthplace, and his wife, Athens. Her parents hailed respectively from Salonica, Greece, and Brindisi, Italy, while the husband's father was born in Smyrna, Turkey, and the mother gave Hebron (now in the state of Trans-Jordan) as her birthplace. They would have been astounded to hear that one parent was a Greek, another an Italian, a third a Turk, and the fourth an Arab. To this rich family of high culture, living in Egypt, it was self-evident that they were all

25

Jews, geographically located in various countries on the shores of the Mediterranean Sea.

The mere existence of the state of Israel will clarify the position of the Jew as a patriot in each country to which he pledges allegiance. Anyone whose national appeal prompts him to depart for Israel, becomes an Israeli as a matter of course, in addition to his Jewish religious and spiritual background. His brother, who remains in Europe or America, likewise an adherent of Judaism as his ancestral religion, will maintain a spiritual bond with Israel as strong as that of some Christians with Catholic Rome and the Vatican City State. In the larger human synthesis of a "United Nations," the reverence of a Jew for Israel, as that an American Catholic for the Vatican City, may be no more incongruous than the double loyalty of one American to the state of New York and others, equally loyal, to the state of California or Texas.

The first Prime Minister of the state of Israel has proclaimed as a legitimate goal: "A Jewish majority in the state of Israel and a majority of Jews (of the world) within that state." The first object is already achieved and safeguarded. The other may be the necessary result of constant persecutions in the Arab states and anti-Semitism in Europe, within a single generation. But always there will remain—as in the days of the Second Temple—a large concourse of Jews outside the narrow limits of the state of Israel. Indeed, "Israel among the nations" remains as a great spiritual post, while the state of Israel is the repository of their ancient traditions and "historic connection" with the heritage of their forefathers.

Judaism, as a religious force, is the only possible spiritual bond between Jews inside and outside of Israel. It

26

serves also as the one great binding force within the state of Israel itself in uniting the various strains stemming from Poland, Russia, Roumania and Germany with the diverse elements from Yemen, Morocco, Iran and Persia. Indeed, when one observes the mingling of the blond types of Eastern and Central Europe with the darker visages from Asia and North Africa, the problem of race and religion becomes of paramount importance.

Often the lighter-skinned European Jew, settled in Israel, must ask himself the question: What have I in common with the dark-haired, darker-skinned newcomers from the Arab countries of the Near and Middle East? For a thousand years and more the history of these groups have diverged along different paths—so distinct and separate as to foster a feeling of racial difference. The wonder grows that such diverse groups can be unified, until the answer comes, clear and unmistakable: only through the devotion to a common religion, its faith of pure monotheism, proclaiming the Fatherhood of God and the Brotherhood of Man, and its tenets based upon the ancient Torah.

It is the still, small voice of the Old Testament from Moses to the prophets of Israel that bids well to become the cementing force for a united Israel in the land of our forefathers. Indeed, but for the memorable history from the Five Books of Moses down to the prophecies of Isaiah and Jeremiah, there could hardly exist Children of Israel today to inherit and rebuild the old land of Israel. Once again, as in olden times, it is the literary and religious creations of the Jewish people that have preserved and united the various blood streams that make up the Israel of today. And so, without the living memory of the Bible and the Talmud, the centrifugal forces that pull from all the four corners of the earth would be too much for a little state at the far end of the Mediterranean basin.

Perhaps, in the not too distant future, there will also be set up within the boundaries of the old land of Israel a center for Judaism—analogous in some respects to the papacy or the conclave of Cardinals, or a Presbyterian Synod—to which all Jews may turn for authoritative interpretation of the laws and practices of the Jewish religion. Such an institution, known as the Sanhedrin, existed in the days of the Second Temple under the Maccabees, and continued even later under Roman rule. Such an institution might serve, in the future as in the past, as the symbol of Jewish religious unity. Of course, this tribunal would never have political power or influence, and its religious jurisdiction would extend only to those members of the Jewish faith who would voluntarily accept its decrees.

Such an institution is the more necessary because, unlike Catholicism and Protestantism, Judaism embraces a whole system of law—the Jewish way of life—in which the attempt is made to regulate the whole life conduct of the individual with the avowed purpose of upbuilding his moral character. In some sense Judaism might almost be described as a secular religion, based upon Laws of the Torah and interpretations by the Rabbis over a period of two thousand years.

In a very real sense, Judaism is the common law of the Jews. Students of English and American legal history appreciate the full significance of such a common law, developed slowly through many ages by decisions of judges, each judgment resting upon the precedents of prior judgments and opinions, and deriving its binding force mainly from the sanction of the community in the support of its own recognized customs. In this respect, Jewish Law or Judaism bears close analogy to the common law; and as we review the efforts of famous judges to ascertain the opinion of a Coke, Mansfield or Marshall, we are constantly reminded of the great Rabbis who seek their sanctions in the views of Hillel, Jochanan Ben Zaccai and Akiba.

Because of unfavorable extraordinary conditions, the Jewish people have for centuries been unable to continue the natural development of this Jewish common law known as Judaism, its normal course having been interrupted from the time of completion of the Talmud. In the days of the Sanhedrin, the Rabbis and learned laymen met, discussed and analyzed Jewish rules of conduct "in the light of reason," adopting new regulations and modifying old rules in conformity with the just needs of each age. During many centuries, however, Judaism has been deprived of such a law-making and law-interpreting body. As an inevitable result, there has been a stagnation of certain Jewish rules of life conduct against which both reform Judaism and modern conservative Judaism constitute a protest. Unless a Jewish lawmaking and law-interpreting institution is re-established, we shall be forced, in order to escape the bounds of a stagnant religion, to accept a milk-and-water Judaic creed which might restrict its activity within the narrow spheres of Sabbath sermons and Sunday lectures.

The Sanhedrin, on the contrary, was the Parliament where Jewish religious and communal questions were debated and Jewish law determined. In some form such a Sanhedrin, representing the Jews of the world for religious purposes, must be reconstituted on a democratic basis. As a matter of fact, such a Sanhedrin was already foreshadowed when the American Jewish Congress was established, during World War I, under the presidency of Dr. Stephen S. Wise. It has been expanded into a World Jewish Congress. It is now high time that out of these precedents there be developed a democratic institution, modeled after the old Sanhedrin, with seventy-one members, having a permanent seat in the state of Israel and operating not sporadically, at yearly conferences, but as a continuous body, as the protector and guardian of Judaism. Such a Sanhedrin would develop into the effective religious assembly for world Jewry. It would become the direct heir of the glories and traditions of the Sanhedrin of old—the living witness of a united Jewry. Representatives elected from the far corners of the earth would learn to look with pride upon this institution in the land of our forefathers, and quote with renewed fervor the words: "From Zion shall go forth the law and the word of the Lord from Jerusalem."

CHAPTER TWO

Free Land and Free Labor

In the midst of the difficult war year of 1918, American Zionists, in convention assembled under the presidency of Justice Louis D. Brandeis, formulated the Pittsburgh Platform, which may be regarded as the expression of the ideals of social Zionism. That platform, and the actual forms of social enterprise in Jewish Palestine, may yet point the pathway toward social justice in a bewildered world.

The second, third and fourth principles enumerated in this platform are a declaration of social Zionism, as a complement to the political Zionism of the older days:

"2. To insure in the Jewish National Home in Palestine equality of opportunity, we favor a policy which, with due regard to existing rights, shall tend to establish the ownership and control of the land and of all natural resources, and of all public utilities by the whole people.

"3. All land, owned or controlled by the whole people, should be leased on such conditions as will insure the fullest opportunity for development and continuity of possession.

"4. The cooperative principle should be applied as far

31

as feasible in the organization of all agricultural, industrial, commercial and financial undertakings."

The very next year, in preparation for the Peace Conference at Paris, which ended World War I and at which the World Zionist Organization presented its case for a Jewish National Home in Palestine, I drafted a memorandum, embodying a program for land reform which might avoid the speculative rise in land values due to the adoption of the British Mandate over Palestine.

"Concretely, if Great Britain should immediately assume the guardianship of Palestine (as trustee for the future Jewish government), the land in Palestine will immediately increase in value to an enormous extent. This increase would be due solely to the conviction that under British control life and property would be safeguarded and the economic development of the country would be assured. Now this increase in land values would be the direct benefit conferred by the new government, without any help whatsoever from the present-day land owners.

"Therefore, in logic and in justice, this increase in land values ought to be appropriated by the government in the shape of a special land value tax. To achieve such a program of just taxation, the commission which is to administer Palestine should be given the right expressly to assess and value all plots of land as of August 1, 1914 (immediately before the Great War). This Palestine Commission, and, thereafter its successor, the government of Palestine, would then proceed to impose an annual land value tax upon the plots of land under its control, whereby excess unearned value which might have been added to such land since August 1, 1914, exclusive, of course, of all

32

improvements made by the owner or the tenants, would go into the treasury of the government. This would result in giving to the government the values which society itself (as distinguished from the individual landowners) is creating from day to day, while reserving the right of the landowners to the values which they held in the best days that Palestine has known in modern times. Such a system of taxation would eliminate land speculation, since all excess unearned values would go to the government instead of to land speculators.

"In order to understand the full effects of such a system of taxation, we would study the picture that Palestine might present to us if we failed to adopt land value taxation. Present landowners of Palestine who, in the main, have done little to develop the country, would reap a golden harvest from the establishment of a new government and, with the influx of Jews, land values would go sky-high, so that every Jew who migrated to Palestine from Russia, Roumania, or America—a pioneer in the Jewish Renaissance—would be compelled to purchase land at inflated values or pay exorbitant rents, thereby helping to develop a class of absentee Palestinian landlords who would be spending their incomes (obtained from Palestine workers) and idling through days spent in luxurious capitals of the world. In effect, it would be enacting a law for the restriction of Jewish immigration into Palestine, since it would make it difficult for poor Jews to secure land or living quarters on fair terms."

This prediction was justified in the decades between the two World Wars when not only do-nothing Arab landlords, dwelling generally outside Palestine, profitted richly from the rise of land values due to Jewish immigration, but also many Jews, engaged in land speculation, piled up profits from the dire need of their fellow immigrants for land and houses. We must understand that it is not the individual who is at fault, but the system which promotes and encourages unearned profits from increasing land values in a growing community. Taxation may do much to mitigate this evil, so well illustrated in the old story of the Turkish tax upon olive trees. There, the tax was first so high that the peasants soon gave up the planting of olive trees as unremunerative. Accordingly, the government received no taxes, and the peasants had no olives. But later a wise Governor arrived and placed a reasonable tax upon the acreage irrespective of whether it was planted with trees; so the peasants were forced to plant olive trees in order to be able to meet the tax. To their surprise, not only did the government receive its maximum in taxes, but the peasants found sufficient surplus to justify their investment of time and labor.

Moreover, much can be done to correct the evils of land speculation by a tax system which bears lightly upon producers and more heavily upon those who hold the title deeds to land. But far better than any tax system is the simple proposition that the public must preserve the ownership, particularly of urban lands, so rapidly increasing in value. The result of such increase of land value would then benefit the whole population, including farmers as well as city dwellers.

The land of Israel, in the twenty years preceding World War II, paid a heavy price to land speculators for the growth of cities such as Tel Aviv and Haifa. The Jewish National Fund, established by the Zionist Organization as early as 1903 to acquire real estate as the inalienable property of the whole Jewish people, did as much as it could do to protect the population, particularly the settlers in cooperative farm colonies, but in those days that institution was too weak financially to ameliorate the condition of the town dwellers, who suffered much from rising rents and inadequate living accommodations. The only sure method to safeguard the rights of the tenants as well as the community against the proverbial greed of land speculators, is to eliminate the element of speculation itself by preserving the ground rent for the benefit of the public as a whole.

Unfortunately, this just program was made impossible at that time because the British government, perhaps correctly, feared the opposition of the entrenched Arab landlord class who were so influential that they might have fomented a rebellion under the guise of a nationalist revolution. Accordingly, Palestine suffered from a series of land speculation booms during the interval between the two world wars; by boosting land prices far beyond their real value, they burdened the whole economy. I remember discussing this whole problem with Justice Brandeis, on our return trip from Palestine, soon after the termination of World War I. He favored wholeheartedly such a just program of land taxation, but concluded that, as a practical measure, it might be difficult to introduce it over Arab opposition. I recall his memorable words almost verbatim: "There are times when it is too difficult to reach the top of a hill by climbing straight upward. In that case, you must cut a circular path with a gradual slope, climbing slowly upward, until you can reach the top. We must buy the land, and by a coordinated policy of land purchase, particularly through the Jewish National Fund, we shall finally attain the goal."

In short, this program of land reform which might have saved, for the benefit of all the people of Palestine, Arabs as well as Jews, the annual income from hundreds of millions of dollars (it went, instead, into the pockets of land speculators, both Jewish and Arab) became impossible, because of the lack of foresight of a primitive people and the selfish opposition of a small Arab landlord class.

But this is not merely the story of "what might have been," because we have it yet in our power to correct the mistakes of the past. The value of the land alone (exclusive of improvements) of the rocky island of Manhattan has been assessed for tax purposes by the City of New York as worth more than $4 billion—a little over three centuries since this island was purchased from the Indians for trinkets worth about $24. Who can estimate the benefits that might have accrued to the people of the City of New York if the early Dutch settlers had firmly resolved to keep this as an inalienable estate to be leased to individual citizens, who would be charged ground rent, periodically reassessed on the basis of its increasing capital value?

This is no new radical doctrine, but good capitalist procedure, as well exemplified in the story of the leases made by Columbia University on the grounds upon which the Rockefeller Center now proudly stands in the City of New York. In 1814, the state of New York gave this farm land, stretching from present-day 48th Street to 51st Street on Fifth Avenue, with a width of one large block, as a donation to help maintain Columbia College as an institution of learning. A long succession of wise trustees kept this land as the "inalienable property" of Columbia University and resisted the temptation to sell the estate during the hard times and depressions that have occurred periodically nearly every other decade since that time. Finally, they were able to lease the site of this old farm, in 1928, for a net annual rental of $3.5 million, with the added provision that the ground rental would be reassessed every twenty-one years on the basis of 5 per cent of the capital value of the land, upon which there have now been erected immense structures at a cost of over $100 million. The lease, now running for a term of ninety-six years, has proven highly satisfactory not only to Columbia University, but equally to the Rockefeller interests, who were able to use the funds that might have been immobilized in land purchase for building operations which have proven highly profitable.

Such long and favorable leases on land constitute no restriction upon private enterprise but, on the contrary, make it possible for private interests to utilize large sums of money, which might otherwise have been bottled up in sterile land, for productive building purposes. In like manner, large chain store organizations like the Woolworth Company prefer to lease their store sites for a long period, and thereby are enabled to utilize the cash, otherwise unproductive in "dead real estate," for constantly expanding their organization—opening new stores for the benefit both of their stockholders as well as consumers. From the point of view of the Rockefeller interests or an organization like Woolworth, it makes little difference whether Columbia University or private individuals hold the title, or some city or state is the rent-collecting landlord. But from the point of view of society as a whole, it is certainly highly desirable that an institution of learning should reap the advantages from the increased land values rather than some speculating landlord.

By the time the state was established in May, 1948, the rural holdings of the Jewish National Fund had reached the figure of 942,000 dunam (235,000 acres), and, six years later, the total area under Jewish National Fund ownership was approximately 3,500,000 dunam (nearly a million acres) upon which there lives a population of approximately 500,000 Jews.

Because the Jewish National Fund was forced to concentrate upon redeeming the soil of Israel essential for agricultural purposes, it had to forego, in large measure, the possibility of acquiring urban lands, where the rent income is so much greater. Unfortunately, in the early days before World War I, the importance of securing control over city land was hardly realized. It may be recalled that as early as 1909, the land area upon which the original township of Tel Aviv was established had been purchased with the funds and guarantees of the Jewish National Fund (for about $50,000). However, instead of holding this valuable estate as a public domain, titles to the land were transferred to individuals which, if retained as a public trust, might have yielded a rent income, over the last generation, sufficient to have placed Israel on the road to achieving the social program announced in the Pittsburgh Platform.

Early in 1949, only nine months after the establishment of the state of Israel, some of us, thinking in terms of social Zionism, turned again to the problem of land redemption, and the Hebrew and English press in Jerusalem and Tel Aviv carried articles in which it was proposed

38

that a substantial bond issue be marketed for the express purpose of purchasing the urban land in the rapidly growing cities of Israel, which then would be leased back to the former landlords on a ground rental basis. This would have assured to the infant state a constantly increasing revenue for economic development and the protection and safeguarding of its currency. Unfortunately, although the suggestion was favorably received, with friendly comments, the whole matter was passed over in view of the harsh necessities arising from the armistice agreement with the Arab states and the immediately pressing demands created by huge immigration in the following years.

At that time it was suggested that the Jewish National Fund issue bonds to effect such a land redemption program that would carry interest at the rate of 4 per cent. A simple table will show that within a period of approximately twenty-eight years all the bonds would be paid off, if only 6 per cent of the original price of such city lands were so appropriated, and accumulated each year for the payment of interest and redemption of the bonds. As the Jewish National Fund would come into the possession of the land immediately, we can be certain that the average income in rents from such municipal lands would be in excess of 6 per cent, because of the periodic increases in land values and rents. Two per cent each year would be utilized as a sinking fund for the redemption of the bonds, as shown in the last column, and 4 per cent as interest on the bonds. For convenience, in calculating the interest, more than $50 was regarded as equivalent to $100 and less than $50 as equivalent to zero. After twenty-eight years, the payment of only $3,000 on each $1,000,000 would clear the entire debt by 1977.

In the following table, outstanding bonds for $1,000,000 were taken as convenient figures. The figures below would be multiplied by the number of million dollars of assessed valuation of such urban land, exclusive of improvements. If the plan had been adopted, as suggested in 1950, we might already have been well on our way to the redemption of the soil of Israel, as the table on page 41 will show.

However, it is not too late, even now, to secure the chief benefits in another, and perhaps better, form. We need merely extend the program of the Jewish National Fund—now so largely engrossed in the acquisition of agricultural land—likewise to urban lands, where land speculation is always a threat and a danger. It is in the acquisition of such city lands that the program of land reform may yield highly fruitful results. Under such a program, the Jewish National Fund would agree to purchase any and all urban lands (exclusive of improvements thereon) that may be offered during a period of a year or two at the prices fixed by the Government Land Registrar. Such property would immediately be leased back by the Jewish National Fund to the seller, on the basis of a net rent of 6 per cent per annum to the Jewish National Fund. (Since interest rates are relatively high in the new state of Israel, such a ground rental is eminently fair and reasonable.) The credit standing of the Jewish National Fund is so high that a 4 per cent internal bond issue, amortized over a period of twenty-eight years, to cover such purchases could readily be negotiated, even without the guarantee of the state. But by a lasting agreement between the state and the Jewish National Fund, the former could very well undertake such a guarantee on

40

	AMOUNT OF BONDS OUTSTANDING	INTEREST	BONDS REDEEMED
1950	$1,000,000	$40,000	$20,000
1951	980,000	39,200	20,800
1952	959,200	38,400	21,600
1953	937,600	37,500	22,500
1954	915,100	36,600	23,400
1955	892,700	35,700	24,300
1956	868,400	34,700	25,300
1957	843,100	33,700	26,300
1958	816,800	32,700	27,300
1959	789,500	31,600	28,400
1960	761,100	30,400	39,600
1961	731,500	29,300	30,700
1962	700,800	28,000	32,000
1963	668,800	26,800	33,200
1964	635,600	25,400	34,600
1965	601,000	24,000	36,000
1966	565,000	22,600	37,400
1967	527,600	21,100	38,900
1968	488,700	19,500	40,500
1969	488,200	18,000	42,000
1970	406,200	16,200	43,800
1971	362,400	14,500	45,500
1972	316,900	12,700	47,300
1973	269,600	10,800	49,200
1974	220,400	8,800	51,200
1975	169,200	6,800	53,200
1976	116,000	4,600	55,400
1977	60,600	2,400	57,600

the understanding that the ground rents so received by the Jewish National Fund would be utilized, in the first instance, as a firm protection for Israel's currency.

Leases for ground rent made by the Jewish National

41

Fund now run for a period of forty-nine years and are renewable for a similar term, but the ground rent would be readjusted periodically (let us say, every fourteen years in each period) so as to secure for the benefit of the public the increase in land value, as in the case of the Columbia leases for Rockefeller Center.

It seems to me that now is the proper time for the inauguration of such a program. Land values have fallen due to the new economic policy leading toward currency stabilization. Landlords are now pressed for ready cash, and a large majority would be ready and willing to sell their holdings for reasonable prices offered by the Jewish National Fund, especially if they would have the opportunity still to hold possession of their lands as leasehold estates. No element of government coercion would be involved; yet it is certain that purely on a voluntary basis the major portion of the urban lands would speedily pass under the control of the Jewish National Fund.

The advantages offered to landlords in converting their lands into ground rent leases from the Jewish National Fund would be so great that there would undoubtedly be a rush of applicants to change their holdings into cash, which would enable the owners to erect valuable buildings upon their leasehold estates, or otherwise improve their lands with profit to themselves.

Within a single generation, the Jewish National Fund would in this way become the unencumbered owner of most of the urban lands within the boundaries of the state of Israel. At the same time, the public generally would become the permanent beneficiary of the increasing land values for all future time. It may be that in a few cities the ground rent might occasionally fall below the 6 per cent required to meet interest and amortization on some parcels of real estate. Then the Jewish National Fund, controlling the largest part of the urban lands, would easily be able to make up the loss from the increased value in other sectors, for it is inconceivable that city land as a whole would decrease in value in an expanding new country in the early days of its industrial development.

The net result would be the certainty of great public benefits from the income from ground rents within a single generation. It would also mean that the city population would be able, in greater measure, to control the growth and character of the urban lands, rather than leave it at the mercy of greedy landlords and the unregulated influx of tenants. We can anticipate that, under Jewish National Fund auspices, the public would receive the benefit of parks, playgrounds and boulevards (since it would not be forced to compensate the property owners) and what the city might lose by the creation of breathing places in one congested locality might very well be gained in increasing rents from surrounding districts. The money and time now often expended on the establishment of a small park in a congested district might well be saved for further important projects for the general welfare.

I am saying nothing here about any plan for the purchase of farmers' holdings, since such increases in land value are moderate and reasonable and seldom the result of speculation, and especially so in Israel where the Jewish National Fund operates to protect the actual tiller of the soil by granting long-term hereditary leaseholds. It is only when such land is not already under the control of the Jewish National Fund and about to be converted into industrial sites, or utilized for commercial purposes, that the Jewish National Fund would step in to acquire the ground rights, with full compensation thereof. Such chance rewards as the individual farmer might receive from increased value of his land may be regarded as a just reward for his past steadfastness and a mark of appreciation by the nation toward those engaged in raising its necessary food supply. The public can afford to be generous in such cases, so long as we make it impossible for any small group of landlords to become the masters of a fast-growing commercial center like Tel Aviv or a port city like Haifa. By legal enactment of the state of Israel, the mineral resources are already protected for the benefit of the public, for the subsoil rights belong to the state (licenses being granted to companies and individuals for exploration and exploitation). Only the control of the urban lands by the Jewish National Fund would safeguard the still larger income from ground rent for the benefit of the public.

Present-day owners of vacant or unimproved lands would be the first to avail themselves of opportunities to secure fresh capital to defray the cost of substantial improvements, enabling them to hold this increasingly valuable real estate under long-term leases from the Jewish National Fund. Indeed, instead of inert capital tied up in sterile land—similar to the capital that was tied up in the bodies of Negro slaves before the American Civil War—there would be an impetus to utilize the freshly released capital (from the Jewish National Fund Bond issue) for capital improvements, thereby increasing employment and encouraging industrial expansion. No other

44

single measure could give such a lift to the whole economy of Israel for, while directly benefiting the building industry, the new available capital indirectly would encourage agricultural production as well as commerce and manufacture.

To those who may object that such large income from ground rent would make the Jewish National Fund too wealthy, we need only point out that it is a public body and will always be dependent upon public opinion and, therefore, must operate for the benefit of the public generally. With such a substantial public income from ground rents, represented by ever-increasing urban property values, there would be less reason, and no excuse, to extend state activities to a point where an overbearing bureaucracy might operate to discourage private enterprise.

As an alternative to a minutely regulated communist state, America has produced in the last century the important philosophical concept arising from the land reform program of Henry George. Far more significant than the particular method of land taxation with which his name is associated, is the concept of a self-regulated industrial system as its necessary consequence. Over and above any value that may be attached to the peculiar system of a Single Tax program is the view of an industrial system that regulates itself. Far removed from political coercion and applying a method of voluntary adjustment that seeks the sanction of those who fear the coercive power of the state, this is the very antithesis of communism, for in the place of the collectivism of the latter, with its emphasis on state activity, the followers of Henry George would rather enshrine the principles of individual initiative and private enterprise. Once the individual is freed from the threat of private land monopoly, the necessity for extensive state interference no longer exists.

It may seem strange that the Socialist Labor Party, which was in control of the government of Israel in its first full decade, failed to pay proper attention to the vital land problem. But socialists have been proverbially blind to the important issue which Henry George so vigorously presented. Perhaps we should say that they are often so blinded in their battle over "capitalism" that they refuse to grasp the significance of the "unearned increment" from land, which is generally the root evil of a particularly vicious kind of "capitalism." But it is historically true that even in Great Britain, where Henry George had a substantial following, including such important members of the Fabian Society as George Bernard Shaw and Sidney Webb, the Labor Party, nevertheless, took no decided stand on the land issue—and the famous Lloyd George Budget of 1910, somewhat limiting land profits, was allowed quietly to die. On the other hand, the communists in Russia by expropriating the land have destroyed the farmers' incentives to produce the maximum food. This was the result of a failure to recognize the distinction between urban land, which can be most profitably nationalized without curbing individual initiative, and rural lands, which require all the efforts of the state to encourage the most profitable utilization. Fortunately, we may still profit from the lesson of the past—and the public ownership of urban lands in Israel can, and will, meet with the approval of all the major political parties.

The Pittsburgh platform enshrined by American Zionists, in a unanimous vote of the convention in 1918, as a goal for the future Jewish state, thus forms the bridge with the old order program of the Jewish National Fund as the proper pathway for the state of Israel.

This discussion may well end with the wise injunction of Spinoza, "The fields and the whole soil and (if it can be managed) the houses should be public property—let at yearly rental to the citizen."

CHAPTER THREE

A Labor Commonwealth

In the early days of American history, the unemployed, by moving to the unexplored fields of the West, constituted themselves into small, self-sufficient economic units, in this way effectively regulating the labor market. The manufacturing establishments and the commercial enterprise, before 1880, had to compete with the open fields of the West in securing their supply of labor. As a result, this free land not only solved the problem of the unemployed, but also assured the establishment of a relatively high standard of living and the "American wage" which made it possible. The free lands of the West automatically fixed a rough minimum wage for labor by placing a limit below which the wage earner would rather work as a squatter or free settler in the unoccupied country of the West.

But Israel is like an old, settled country, in which no free land is available, and where we must constantly face the problem not only of unemployment, but also of a living wage for the worker. Is there any substitute for the free lands of the American West as a solution for the problem of unemployment and a minimum wage? Unless such an effective method is found, we may periodically be confronted, in every economic crisis or depression, with conditions that foster economic and even political revolutions—when able-bodied and willing workers may be starving because of the lack of opportunities for labor.

By a curious history, in the first decade before World War I, such an alternative method to meet the old problem of unemployment was developed by the second wave (Aliyah) of Jewish immigrants into a benighted land, then ruled by the Turkish Sultan, but known from ancient times as the "Land of Promise." These pioneers, rebels against the tyranny of the Russian Tsars, were filled with enthusiasm for a socialist brotherhood, in which all would be equal workers upon a soil owned by the people as a whole. Fortunately, fate was propitious for such an enterprise in the early days of the twentieth century, for the Zionist organization, seeking a "legally assured home" for the Jewish people, had established the Jewish National Fund, dedicated to the purpose of purchasing land in Palestine to be held as the inalienable property of the Jewish people. Even those who did not subscribe to the doctrine of socialism were willing to allow an experiment of Jewish cooperative labor upon land purchased with the pennies gathered from the Jewish masses all over the world—land which these immigrant groups might occupy as tenants upon the inalienable estate of the Jewish people.

The Jews who came to Palestine half a century ago were peculiarly equipped to grapple with this age-old problem of unemployment and poverty. Three thousand years of education, while they were imbibing the words of the prophets of Israel, have predisposed all Jews to the precepts of social justice. Now in the land of Israel, they were experimenting on fertile ground, freed from the hostile environment to which they were formerly subjected.

From this point of view, it is distinctly worthwhile to examine carefully the cooperative farm settlement system of the labor colony known as the Kvutzah, established upon the land of the Jewish National Fund, for the ultimate solution of the problem of unemployment and poverty. The basis of membership in the Kvutzah is entirely voluntary, in contrast both to the enforced cooperation of the impoverished subjects of a Soviet Union or the regimented efforts of some coercive fascist regime. No one is under any compulsion to join the Kvutzah cooperative settlement and any member may withdraw, to live once again in the competitive arena of modern economic society. But to every Jew in Israel, there is the ever-present opportunity to abandon the field of private competition and join in one of the numerous agricultural cooperative farm settlements, usually holding from one hundred to four hundred members, who live by the principle of "equal pay for all" out of the proceeds of their cooperative farming effort. Some of these farm colonies have extended their operations to include small factory units, a textile mill or a brick factory, and some have even acquiesced in permitting their members to work as city laborers in a nearby town, but all receive equally the food, clothing and shelter necessary for decent living, with especially fine quarters and schools for children, while communal health measures guarantee every individual the best of care in sickness and convalescence.

In like manner, these farm colonies on the hills of Galilee, or in the Vales of Sharon, constitute an institution which inevitably operates to protect not only the unemployed, but even those who are employed, from the worst ravages of a harsh, competitive system that so often discards many unemployed as unfit. Just so long as we have a large class of laborers who are forced into the ranks of the unemployed, in any recurrent economic crisis, without the opportunity of earning a decent livelihood, so long must they act as a handicap on our whole industrial system. Being dismissed from the regular industrial army, they become the scum of the labor market, forced to accept the lowest wages sufficient to hold body and soul together. By their unwholesome competition with the more reliable labor force, they tend to force down the wages of all. The mere presence in the industrial market of a large class of jobless men, who must somehow find food, clothing and shelter is a destructive force that operates to reduce the efficiency of the whole economy.

The Kvutzah system of cooperation in farming settlements was originally planned rather as a training school for agriculture, so as to convert gradually the erstwhile town dwellers into a reliable farming class. But even in the early days, after Dagania and Kinnereth were established in the Jordan Valley, in 1909, it was recognized that these pioneers had literally stumbled upon a great economic principle: the development of cooperative settlements which might offer an alternative to those who fail to find employment within our competitive system of industry.

To the surprise of many critics, it was soon discovered that the love for Mother Earth was just as strong in the former town dweller of Eastern European ghettoes, known as the Russian Pale of Settlement, as in the typical peasant of France or Germany. Where the Jew had been deliber-

51

ately denied access to the soil, he was literally forced to pick up the peddlers' pack or to eke out a meager living as a petty tradesman. But as an immigrant to the old land of Israel, the attractive call of a farmer's life became so great in the score of years that formed the interval between the two world wars that nearly every Jewish workingman in Tel Aviv, Haifa or Jerusalem planned for the happy days when he would be able to "return" to the soil, if not as an independent farmer, at least as a member of the Kvutzah.

It soon became evident that this system of communal farming went far beyond the program of a mere training school for future farmers. It operated in the past also as an effective social institution for draining off the unemployed from the towns—a process far more efficient economically than the wasteful method of providing public works. At the same time, these farming settlements served as a rough guarantee for a minimum wage among the workers as a whole, since the laborer could refuse to accept an unfair wage and join, as an alternative, one of the collective farms where at last food and shelter were collectively assured. Even in those early days, it seemed obvious that these simple workingmen (like their precursors of the Rochdale experiment in England) had made a great economic discovery, which might later prove of inestimable value on a larger scale. The laudable efforts of the state of Israel to divert as many as possible recent immigrants to these farm colonies, with the example set by its dynamic first Prime Minister, David Ben-Gurion, offered the prospect that the Kvutzah system would become an integral part of the Israel economy and set a model for the world at large.

The spectacle of a Prime Minister retiring from active service to join a labor cooperative farm (and only called back to his post in a political emergency fraught with the danger of war and the consequent Sinai campaign) will long remain a symbol of devotion not only to the state but to the ideal of social brotherhood. The state of Israel is deliberately inculcating that ideal by offering every immigrant the prospect of becoming a member in a cooperative farm colony—with freedom to return to the competitive system of industry at any time.

In short, these farming settlements are fostered by the state to attract all those who are willing to forego the opportunities within the competitive system, in exchange for the security and comforts of life in a Kvutzah cooperative settlement.

The principle upon which these farm labor cooperatives rest in the land of Israel is: Every man is entitled to work and to receive for his labor the physical necessities of existence: the bread, shelter and clothing which nature demands. All the luxuries of life may be acquired by those on the outside who are more successful in the industrial struggle for existence, but also with adequate provision for all within these cooperative farming settlements. The effect of such an arrangement must be not to eliminate competition from our industrial system but rather to raise its plane: to substitute for the merciless struggle of the poor for bread and shelter, the more inviting struggle of well-fed men for the luxuries, pleasures and honors of life. Such farming cooperative colonies will automatically fix a minimum wage below which the struggle for existence will not be permitted to sink.

One might urge, with some semblance of justice, that

the establishment of such self-sufficient farming settlements would simply mean reversion to the earlier forms of economic development and, therefore, this might be condemned as an attempt to substitute for a world market of industry a comparatively simple form known even to the ancients. Such an argument implies that we have made great progress in economics during the last century and a half.

No one would voluntarily surrender the gains already secured. But we must not blind ourselves to the danger of unemployment and poverty that seem to go hand in hand with every crisis in advancing civilization. We too often assume that progress is synonymous with complexity—in economic organization as in social life. But complexity, in and of itself, is not progress, although it usually accompanies true progress. However, progress must not be bought at the price of unemployment or poverty, and if the program of self-sufficient cooperative labor colonies be viewed as a cry of "back to nature," then it might be justifiable to go back even to the primal forms of economic organization in order to safeguard society and protect the citizen from poverty and unemployment. In short, a system of cooperative farm colonies offers the opportunity of testing progress, of ascertaining the value of our complex economic system.

These settlements will prove at the same time the barometer and safety valve of our industrial system. They indicate the amount of pressure on the labor surplus, sometimes designated as the "submerged tenth," and offer a land vacuum where the unemployed may earn their own living by the sweat of their brows. Furthermore, such farming settlements serve as a measure of true progress in our economy, and indicate just how many workers are discarded by our economic system from time to time. They offer the so-called "unfit"—the men who are unable to adjust themselves to our economic system—a haven of refuge in self-sufficient farming colonies. If this be regarded as a retrogression, then the answer is plain that we reserve such farming settlements only for those who have found no place in our progressive societies. In effect, we place a limit on our present-day industrial system only insofar as it may be necessary to abolish poverty and eliminate unemployment. Such farm colonies will prove to be the protective tariff wall for all laborers, for they will eliminate from competitive industry only those wage earners who furnish the nucleus for revolution in the periodical recessions, while unemployed. And to those who reject the competitive system, the farming colonies offer the alternative of employment in a cooperative society that will insure to each member at least the necessities of life.

But the Jew is first and foremost an individualist and even his socialist predilections should be attributed to a demand for social justice rather than to a mere expression for the search for personal security. So it is not surprising that before long there was a reaction to the strict doctrine of the Kvutzah, and there developed side by side a variant of a cooperative farm settlement known as the Moshav, in which individual initiative is allowed full play. Thus, while the Moshav is a cooperative group in its dealings with the outside—its foreign affairs, so to speak—it permits individual holdings of leased lands, so that each family can profit from its own initiative and hard work. The Moshav cooperative sells and buys collectively for the settlement, selling the products for all its members, but each member receives the full rewards for his efforts in proportion to the produce that he turns in to the "treasury" of the Moshav. It is not surprising to learn that the Moshav has so far outstripped the Kvutzah in members and strength and that it is particularly favored by the more recent immigrants. Yet together the two forms are complementary efforts in protecting the economy of Israel and safeguarding the cooperative way of life.

But the Moshav as well as the Kvutzah constitute a far cry from the system of Chinese communes, because they rest on a voluntary basis, with freedom for every member to withdraw and live within the competitive system of industry as a free workingman or farmer.

Such a system of farm-labor cooperatives is, in essence, a voluntary cooperative society, organized not to exclude individual initiative from the competitive system of industry, but rather to raise the plane of the present system based upon private profit. These farm-labor cooperatives, organized on a voluntary basis, will result in establishing a proper balance between the competitive system of industry, based upon profit, and the communal settlements, offering protection to all those who prefer, or are forced, to live outside the competitive system. It will save for modern society the invaluable factor of individual initiative and yet enable us to regulate such a system by the voluntary withdrawal of the surplus unemployed.

Neither minimum wage laws nor organization of labor unions can solve the ever-recurring problem of unemployment, and this is due to conditions inherent in our competitive system of industry itself—which cannot be eliminated, except by the establishment of some institution outside of the competitive economic system of our day. So long as science and industrial management often make it possible for nine men to do the work necessary for the support of ten and *we make no proper adjustment for utilizing the labor of the tenth man,* we must have periods of adjustment and acute unemployment. Our problem is to find a place for this tenth man.

Now if we offer this "marginal" working man the necessities of life outside of the economic system, we automatically solve the problem not only of unemployment, but also of a minimum wage. Instead of restrictive laws and useless struggles between capital and labor, we need some such effective institution which shall supply work and a living wage in farm cooperative settlements in order to humanize our industrial system. This will not eliminate competition, but raise its plane by offering opportunities for a living wage outside of the competitive system of industry—just as the open fields of the West in early American history effectively regulated the problem of unemployment and its inevitable consequence, poverty.

The Kvutzah system of farm-labor cooperatives in Israel is the crowning achievement of the Histadruth, or Labor movement, in that country. It bears a message that will encircle the globe, for it is worldwide in its significance. It represents a system of "voluntary socialism" which will help to make our modern economic system self-regulating. The whole gamut of our economic thinking, throughout the ages, oscillates between the extreme laissez-faire competition and the communist principle of coercive cooperation. Both competition and cooperation find their counterparts in nature—as Darwin in his *Origin of the*

57

Species with its "Survival of the Fittest," and Kropotkin in his "Mutual Aid," so convincingly prove.

In economic life, the problem always hinges upon the line of demarcation between competition and cooperation. If we accept the logical deductions from the premise of individualism, we may obtain a society in which "each man's hand will be against his brother," and in which we might succeed in developing a few supermen by sacrificing the great mass and abrogating the rules of morality and ethics. On the other hand, if we endorse the theories of collectivism, we may obtain a social system in which mediocrity will be synonymous with virtue, and economic slavery may go hand in hand with the outward forms of political democracy.

In a combination of competition with cooperation, Israel is developing an economic system from which the whole world may profit. Both competition and cooperation are necessary in the development of a model state. Competition develops strong men, but it offers no guarantee that these fit men will not destroy society and undermine morality by a ceaseless war among the strong. Cooperation acts as a preservative force without, however, any constructive attempts at a selective process. As individualism spells selection, even so collectivism connotes preservation. Competition assures progress, while cooperation aims at race conservation. It is only when we have a proper union between these two forces that we are able to build a society which will not be sacrificed at the behest of individual progress, while the conservation of the species will harmonize with self-development.

Competition and cooperation are both abundantly illustrated in nature, and they must both be utilized by man, if he is to achieve the highest ends of life. The proportion of these two great forces should present an arrangement whereby each society, state or nation would adopt at least that amount of cooperation which will secure a level below which the competitive struggle for existence will not be permitted to sink.

A scholastic philosopher of the Middle Ages might have drawn some important deductions from the acts of the Almighty, as recorded in the Old Testament. When the Children of Israel went forth from Egypt, they wandered for forty years in the desert, supported directly by the bounty of the Lord. The Almighty understood that a nation of slaves can be converted into free men only after they shall have become independent of the tyranny of physical wants. In His beneficent wisdom, He sent them manna from the heavens, to satisfy the craving for food so that His chosen people might have leisure and the inclination to pursue higher things. God knew that the Exodus, in and of itself, could not convert slaves into free men— that liberty means more than mere emancipation, more than the mere negative process of breaking old chains. True liberty is a positive concept; and only after the countrymen of Moses had been freed from the inexorable physical needs, were they really free to follow the Laws announced from Mount Sinai. From such historical facts, a religious philosopher might have justly concluded that the first and primary function of government, as revealed to us through the works of the Lord, must be to endeavor continuously to provide for the physical wants of its citizens. Only after we have removed the despotism created by famine and ill health can we succeed in building a higher self, a better and nobler type of man.

It may seem unnnecessary to provide for farm collectives in days of prosperity, when every able-bodied worker can find his secure place in the industrial system, but the sad experience since the introduction of the factory system, over two centuries ago, has proven that some worldwide depression, with its concomitant stress of severe unemployment, occurs periodically almost every other decade. These cooperative farm colonies are the insurance premium that we must pay to protect the less fortunate in the struggle for existence, and as a safeguard for the social system itself against the dangerous upheavals that may result from the discontent of able-bodied unemployed.

In that respect, Israel may well teach a salutary lesson to the peoples of the West against the days of adversity that so often follow extended periods of prosperity.

CHAPTER FOUR

Public Corporations
Versus State Monopoly

In the preceding chapter, I pointed to the Kvutzah cooperative colonies organized on the principle of "voluntary socialism" as a corrective to the modern economic system based upon profit, so that no wage earner might ever lack food or shelter which he might obtain as a member in the cooperative group of farmers, earning his bread by the tilling of the soil. This must be a minimum requirement in any just economic system that deserves to survive.

But there is always the danger that opponents of so-called capitalist economy may often go much further and demand state monopolies in various industries, with the plausible argument that private monopolies may otherwise be established to the detriment of the public as a whole. Now, perhaps the largest element in the growth of any private monopoly is the control of natural resources, such as mineral rights over oil, iron and coal beneath the surface, and the increasingly valuable urban land. But by exercising public control of this unearned wealth, the growth of private monopolies is effectively restricted. The rights of every new competitor to an equal struggle for

61

economic existence will be assured, and private monopoly will be denied the power to grow by "what it feeds upon."

There will always be, of course, certain necessary public monopolies—such as the general post office; but how far the state should enter into the field of economic life of the people is perhaps the most difficult question that continually vexes the mind of the political philosopher. The state with an extreme "lassez-faire" policy might invite the rule of the clever and unscrupulous in the industrial world, just as in the savage state of nature we have the dominion of the physically strong. But the alternative to a complete laissez-faire policy is not necessarily socialism, which implies the use of coercion by governmental authority. Somewhere between socialism and the theory of laissez-faire lies the happy middle course which will secure the greatest freedom for the individual at the present time. Just what constitutes this course is the question that often divides political parties in nearly every civilized country.

Indeed, the history of the last century and a half shows repeated efforts made, decade after decade, to define the scoop of state interference. Each age endeavors to settle this question according to its own lights—only to find it reversed in succeeding years. For the question of state interference must ever remain a problem for each generation to solve anew, guided by its own light under the peculiar conditions of the times. There is no charmed circle around "individual rights," which may not be crossed by state interference. Liberty is not a static term but a dynamic concept—"a path of progress." Individual liberty is not a negative term, but a positive power; and the state may do much to enhance that power by enlarging opportunities and removing the burdens from the less fortunate in the struggle for existence.

While there is, of course, a sphere of individual activity into which the state must not intrude, this is not a fixed territory, but something that must be determined from time to time, in answer to the question: What is it necessary for the state to do or abstain from doing in order to achieve, for all its citizens, the greatest possible amount of true individual liberty? What is "true individual liberty"? Nothing more nor less than opportunity—the largest amount of opportunity for self-development, for bringing forth the best that is in each man for self-realization. The highest form of liberty is the opportunity given to the individual for as complete a development of self as nature will permit under any given set of conditions. As these conditions change, the concept of liberty must receive different interpretations from time to time.

Ritchie, in his valuable discussion of the "Principles of State Interference," gives clear expression to such a view: "The State has not merely the policeman's business of stepping in to arrest the wrongdoer, nor the sole function of ruthlessly enforcing the fulfillment of contracts, whatever these contracts may be and by whomsoever made, but the duty of providing such an environment for individual men and women as to give all, as far as possible, an equal chance of realizing what is best in their intellectual and moral natures."

He criticizes Herbert Spencer for an adherence to a philosophy of extreme laissez-faire. Spencer, he says, confounded two different results. "The other day," says Ritchie, "we were pulling down an old palace and an old prison; today we are building a school and a library."

Laissez-faire is the proper method for securing the first, but may be altogether inappropriate in achieving the second. "Compulsory education," says John Stuart Mill, "may be regarded as interference with the liberty of the parents, but it is interference on behalf of the child."

Gradually, our views on state interference have been transformed. The state is no longer regarded merely as a legal system with an appendix known as a police force, merely to enforce the decrees of a court. We now know that the state, by regulating and controlling our industrial system, may offer us far more liberty than would otherwise be possible. Herbert Spencer pictures the happy freedom of the savage who owes no allegiance to Parliament with its statutes and its senseless interference in the activities of the individual citizen; but a careful critic reminds us that the poor Englishman, living under a government ruled by many volumes of the revised statutes, has far more liberty than the Australian bushman or the savage of the South Seas, who are forever in fear of starvation and murder. Not by casting off all bonds of law, but by increasing state interference for the regulation of our economic life and for increasing the commonwealth can we reach ever closer to true individual liberty. Indeed, poverty, unemployment and all the conditions unfavorable to the physical development of man are inevitable limitations upon true liberty. These are forces of coercion that set bounds to the self-development of the individual, for they deny to many the opportunities for physical and mental growth.

The most hopeful sign of our civilization is the fact that we have a greater amount of capital, a larger surplus with which to satisfy our physical needs, than that of former ages. Civilization and progress are merely the superstructures resting on the foundation of this economic surplus. The beauties of art and the wonders of science are possible because we are freed, to some extent, from the deadening power of physical needs. The aim of society, therefore, should ever be to increase this economic surplus and to endeavor to relieve the individual citizen, so far as possible, from the tyranny of physical needs. In the province of art, religion, morals and taste, the state should seldom interfere; but, at the same time, in order to promote this very freedom and make of it more than a mere hollow phrase, it must do everything possible to encourage the increase of the economic surplus in the nation as a whole, in order to secure the greater freedom of the citizen from the material needs of existence. Socialism and the theory of laissez-faire must be judged solely from the point of view of utility. That economic system is just, equitable and desirable which will enable a nation to realize a larger economic surplus so distributed as to open better opportunities for the fulfillment of the higher desires and interests in the life of the citizen.

From one point of view, indeed, there may be a strong objection to extensive state interference. It is the argument that has been used repeatedly against socialism, for we might simply substitute the coercion of majority rule for the tyranny of private monopoly. However, instead of a system of unlimited state ownership, which might cripple individual initiative, there is the logical alternative of a *voluntary* cooperative society, not to the exclusion of individual initiative, but rather in competition with private enterprise for the development of a model commonwealth.

This principle of competition by public corporations was introduced by Louis D. Brandeis (later Justice of the United States Supreme Court) in the state of Massachusetts over fifty years ago. In 1906, he succeeded in introducing a system of savings bank life insurance under the supervision and control of the state. Justice Brandeis had investigated the insurance rates of the chief companies issuing industrial life insurance policies (i.e., life insurance in which the premiums are paid in small sums at short intervals, usually weekly, to meet the demands of working people). After a careful study of the facts, he concluded that the rates charged were exorbitant. Accordingly, a law was enacted which permitted the savings banks of Massachusetts, under state supervision, to issue life insurance policies, under a uniform plan, in *competition* with the large industrial insurance companies. On June 26, 1907, such a law was passed by the Legislature of Massachusetts and the following results, as publicly announced, followed in short order:

"The monthly premium rates of the policies issued by the savings banks, including dividends (for each policy holder received dividends which would fall to the stockholder in the ordinary stock insurance company) were 32 per cent less even than the *reduced* rates of the industrial companies.

"Most important of all, the competition of savings bank insurance compelled the industrial companies to reduce their rates so that on the average, the rates were reduced by 20 per cent in the first year. This has meant a saving not only to the working people of Massachusetts, for other states followed their example, of many millions of dollars per year."

The above plan advocated and put into effect by Justice Brandeis is far more valuable than the usual experiments in extended state interference in economic life, since the former has no coercive power of a state or government behind it, which might result in crushing individual initiative. The Brandeis plan involves the principle of *public* rather than governmental competition. The state encourages and supervises the savings bank life insurance, but it does not actively engage in competitive industrial activity. If and when such efforts of a public corporation succeed in competition with private enterprise, the benefits accrue to the public as a whole. Yet, such public efforts will have to meet constantly the competition of private individuals and will never be bolstered by the taxation power of the state.

An extension and modification of the Brandeis plan for savings bank life insurance offers a fruitful field for public competition which will be of invaluable aid in the solution of the problem of private monopolies, on the one hand, and the high cost of living, on the other. Indeed, it offers the prospect of the organization of a cooperative society on a *voluntary basis*, far removed from the dangers of either state monopoly or private trusts.

It is in this direction that the state of Israel has been traveling almost without realizing the theoretical implications, and in spite of the professed socialism of its labor leaders. The organization and development of the Solel Boneh, as a vast construction firm, with large capital funds at its disposal, but owned and controlled by the Histadruth

67

or Labor Party, which may and does compete with other private construction firms, is symbolic of the whole trend in the Israel economy. A huge cement plant and a glass factory, similarly owned by the labor organization of Israel, and operated within the competitive system, and even an insurance company, the Hasneh, owned and controlled by the workingmen, and a workers' bank, offer enough proof that the idea of public competition with private initiative is the goal toward which Israel's economy is inevitably moving.

The real problem that remains revolves around the question of state interference. This is the main source of political differences between the leading parties in Israel— the proper government regulation of these vast capital-labor aggregations, so that the real competition is not suppressed but may rather be encouraged for the benefit of the state and its people.

Socialism repeatedly emphasizes the elimination of economic waste by introducing economies inherent in state monopoly, while the labor supply is presumably so regulated as to avoid unemployment and secure for each worker the full reward of his toil. Indeed, the amelioration of the condition of the poor by securing for all a high standard of living, and time and opportunity for healthful recreation, is socialism's chief claim for support from the workingman. Of all the indictments brought against the competitive system of industry, none has been exploited so much as the craving for profit, which is the basis of present-day economic activity. Socialists and social reformers alike have vied with each other in condemning the unscrupulous greed of the "exploiting class."

Yet, admitting the seamy side of the chase for profits,

we dare not blind ourselves to the public benefits and advantages for society as a whole. With all its shortcomings, our competitive system, because of the large fortunes which it makes possible, insures (after deducting the amount necessary for a high standard of living) the maintenance of a large surplus in the hands of people who can have no further use for the capital besides reinvestment—in addition to the substantial portion taken by the state in the form of taxation. But in any system of democratized industry, with the incidental elimination of large fortunes, there will be practically no surplus for investment.

Yet, under a socialist regime the drive for equal dividends that might be received by the citizens from the business of the socialist state, will be largely expended in the pursuit of a higher standard of living, since the fear of want will be removed by the knowledge that a citizen is a member of a socialist state that will supply work and the material necessities of life. In such a system, there can be no strong motive for the accumulation of fortunes, even if the possibility should exist, since every father will feel that his children must find their proper places in the socialist state.

The glaring exception to this rule is the communist drive for military predominance in Soviet Russia, where "butter" is sacrificed for guns. This is made possible only because the masses are deprived of democratic control over their government, thereby placing the state in a position of unstable equilibrium. But this exception proves the rule that communism, with its dictatorship of the proletariat, is not socialism, and points vividly to the essential difference between the two systems.

An economic surplus for the replacement of capital and an increase in the total of investments, depends almost exclusively upon two factors:

(1) the accumulation of savings by the relatively poorer classes; and

(2) the investments by the wealthy classes, after the attainment of a relatively high standard of living.

Neither of these two motives can operate effectively in a socialist state, since the necessity for savings on the part of the poor will be greatly lessened, and there will be none so rich as to enable him to accumulate a substantial surplus after satisfying the diverse wants of an enlightened world and the higher standard of living that socialism would promote.

It is the preservation and increase of the *economic surplus* that is the great problem which must confront every socialist scheme. We cannot depend upon the accumulation of individuals since the very institution of economic equality makes impossible large savings by such individuals. On the other hand, an industrial system organized for profit compels economy and fosters a spirit of thrift that is essential to the accumulation of an economic surplus. It is highly questionable whether the state as a corporation may be able to accumulate such an economic surplus that will be part of the public property. In our modern economic system, coincident with some necessary waste of life and property, we have the evolution of highly effective methods for securing profits in any particular business, due to the keen industrial struggle which compels the utilization of the most effective management in such industries. The crucial question in a socialist state is whether methods equally as effective as in competitive industry can be evolved free from the waste of such industry. I do not see how this can be achieved except through the recognition of *profit as the end and aim of the managers* of the business in a socialist state. Unless profit be made the central feature, there cannot be a strong motive for profitable management in any industry.

There are, of course, many activities in which profitable management is of no real importance—as in handling the police force of a city. In such cases, we may have splendid management without reliance on the factor of profit. But where we consciously seek an economic surplus (where profit is uppermost), we must stimulate the energy of the manager by offering opportunities for sharing profits due to economical management. In short, the socialist corporation would be compelled to pay a portion of its profits to the active managers of the state's business—a practice that must be distasteful to socialist thinkers. Furthermore, the citizen shareholders, by majority vote, would probably select the managers. To suppose anything else would be to eliminate the democratic feature of social democracy. Accordingly, we might have a repetition of political struggles for office and, as such positions would prove lucrative, the whole machinery of political corruption and boss rule might be transferred to the more profitable field of the socialist state.

It is only through a system of *public corporations,* organized on the principle of wide participation of consumers as well as workers, that we may secure the invaluable benefits of a large economic surplus, since in competition with private enterprise the primary element of profitable management will be preserved. This is the kind of voluntary cooperative enterprise, far removed from the coercive powers of a communist state, that is the peculiar feature of Israel economy which even ante-dated the establishment of the state of Israel. It is the great merit of the Labor Party in Israel that it sponsored the development of these large public corporations, in-cluding consumers' cooperatives, which have reached out even beyond workmen's circles into the broad field of the public at large.

The Inertia of Monopoly

A socialist state presents a danger far greater than any question of an economic surplus. The great evils inherent in monopoly are also necessarily present in a socialist state. It is generally known that trusts and monopolistic combines often suppress valuable patents, even when this represents substantial losses to the public, in order to avoid the necessity of making a particular business con-form to the expensive improvements that such patents would require. Larger corporations have often bought up valuable patents, which they refuse to utilize for the benefit of the public simply because it would mean a reorganization of a large portion of their business. On the other hand, in competitive industries of our day, competi-tion itself constantly forces the elimination of old methods and outworn machinery. Like the evolutionary process, competition eliminates from industry the costly ways of doing things and promotes the introduction of machin-ery and methods that are found most fit in the industrial struggle.

The effects of competition reach even farther than to mere methods of production, for the struggle for economic survival is most pronounced in the field of consumption. Our present economic system has been severely criticized because of the constant economic waste that it entails, for example, in the useless advertisements that extol the virtues of various brands from breakfast foods to cigarettes. While such criticism contains a large element of truth, as evidenced by the fact that the great economies that are promised in the organization of some large trust consist in the elimination of useless advertisements and competing sales agents, we must ever remember the other side of the problem. The whole science of economics depends on the postulate that the increase of wants and the greater satisfaction of human needs are most desirable conditions, and form an index to advancing civilization. Now, advertising campaigns, in newspapers, magazines, radio and television are of direct economic value in stimulating wants and evolving new human needs.

We may, of course, adopt the philosophy of Thoreau and conclude that men should have but few material needs, and even those such as may be easily satisfied in primitive fashion. But so long as we accept the fundamental principle of economics, that civilization and enlightenment are concomitant with the increase of desires and the expansion of human wants, we must conclude that advertising expenses have a true value in modern life. In short, a monopolistic organization of an industry, whether public or private, furnishes no sufficient incentive for change and economic improvement, nor for increase in the diversity of the products for consumption, while our present-day competitive system does provide for such change and improvement, however ruthless and costly the methods which may be applied.

The insuperable difficulties, therefore, of any socialist organization of industries are twofold:

(1) the lack of any guarantee for the maintenance and increase of a large economic surplus; and

(2) the dangers inherent in the inertia of monopoly.

While the cooperative farm settlements constitute a necessary system to safeguard a minimum standard of living and insure society against the recurrent crises of unemployment, we must at the same time maintain the competitive system of industry as a protection against the inertia of monopoly and as a guarantee for the accumulation of a larger economic surplus.

This may be achieved without the annoying petty regulations which seem to encompass most states striving toward a socialist ideal. Instead of licenses, permits and the usual currency controls from which Israel has suffered in the first decade of its independence, as have most European countries under socialist labor domination, there is now developing the sound view that the various public corporations, fostered by the Labor Party itself, may give us a good economy in free competition with private enterprise. In general, it may be said that business activity in Israel tends to enlist private capital on the basis of guaranteed income—in the shape of mortgage bonds, debenture issues, or preferred stock—while leaving the control and "equities" in the hands of the management. This is true not only in the case of labor organizations dominating various industries, but also with corporations controlled by middle class investors, such as "Rassco" in the field of real estate and house building, wherein the stock control is vested in a public body known as the Jewish Agency.

Indeed, the Rural & Suburban Settlement Company (familiarly called "Rassco" in Israel) is an excellent example of the economic pathway which the state of Israel has cut out for itself—something which may well serve as an example for the world at large. Organized at the time of the German-Jewish immigration into Israel in the early '30s, consequent upon the rise of Hitlerism, Rassco has provided, at the same time, a source of income for private investors while performing a unique public service in securing homes and farming estates for private individuals. Instead of relying upon the speculative elements of the population to furnish the necessary corporate funds, as common stockholders, the common shares of Rassco (usually nominated founders' shares) are held in the name of a recognized public body, which guarantees the right of investors to preferred dividends, yet secures control of policies in the hands of institutions that have the interest of the public at large.

The same may be said about the Israel Land Development Company, which has been responsible for the development of large urban areas in Haifa, Jerusalem and Tel Aviv, where the founders' shares, like that of Rassco, are held by the Jewish Agency. This virtually assures that the management of such quasi-public enterprises is vested in institutions responsible to the public at large, through the control of the selection of the managing board of directors.

As a matter of fact, management usually controls large aggregations of capital in America, from railroads to mutual insurance companies, and yet it must prove even more advantageous to the public at large if such control is vested in responsible labor or public institutions rather than in an almost irremovable management, which oper-

75

ates through proxies, wherein the average stockholder has generally little to say. In short, the tendency in the state of Israel is for capital to seek its annual return in the shape of interest rather than dividends from public corporations, while risk capital still plays its unique part in the development of new industries and pioneer undertakings. The real contribution that Israel is making to economic theory is the development of public companies or institutions, the main purpose of which is not mere profit making, but rather the protection of the general public in setting a standard with which private enterprise must compete. In such a system, private enterprise has every encouragement in a fair field of competition, while the public at large is protected as a consumer group, and the standard of living safeguarded for producers and consumers alike.

The modern competitive system of industry often gives us a heartless struggle for existence that often entails enormous waste both of profit and human life, while socialism offers us a system of cooperation in production to the exclusion of individual initiative and private enterprise. The latter system would reduce society to the dead level of existence, dangerous to economic progress, because there is no assurance that it will produce an economic surplus essential to enlightened society, while the inertia of a state monopoly might prevent the growth of a better social system.

Our problem is, therefore, to organize the economy so as to avoid some of the gross waste of present-day competition, while at the same time securing a more equitable distribution of wealth without destroying the incentive for gain and material profits. Various attempts have been made to solve this problem by systems of profit sharing.

Omitting the local and incidental causes for the failure of many profit-sharing schemes, there is still this deeper economic and logical reason: the remedy is not coextensive with the evil it is calculated to eliminate. Even if we assume the existence of some successful profit-sharing corporations—huge capital labor trusts, each safeguarding the welfare of its own employees by liberal allowances in profit sharing and high wages—there would still remain a *consumers'* problem due to the high cost necessary to support such combinations of capital and labor. Instead of a labor problem arising out of the condition of the wage earners, we would substitute a consumer problem because of the prohibitive prices imposed by a food capital-labor corporation, a similar clothing trust or a house building monopoly.

To be successful, we must secure some basis for the participation of the *consumers*—the all-embracing class—in the profits of our industrial system. In theory, this is altogether just and proper since, by creating the demand, the consumers constitute the greatest factor in economic value. In practice, the only large cooperative plans that have proven successful are those in which the benefits are distributed in proportion to consumption. The well-known cooperative stores in Great Britain and Scandinavia, sharing their profits in the shape of rebates (or dividends) on the amount and value of the purchases, have been far more successful than any schemes for cooperative manufacture. (In the latter case, cooperation is always a difficult matter because of the manifold problems of efficiency, trade regulations and the struggle for world markets.)

In fact, we may draw the general conclusion that cooperation proves successful only when it tends to be all-inclusive in its membership, and generally fails when it attempts restriction and monopolization. As a further illustration of the truth of this conclusion, we have the successful efforts of the cooperation of farmers in the distribution of their products—particularly worthy of notice is the cooperation in the sale of dairy products by the farmers of Denmark. The farmers share in proportion to the value of the products that each brings to the cooperative sales agency, while they retain the rewards due to personal skill, labor and industry. We have here a successful cooperative business in the *distribution* of products which, by its very nature, is nonrestrictive.

Profit-sharing plans, therefore, to be permanently successful, must be all-inclusive and not confined to the laborers of a particular industry. It is only just and proper that the profits should bring benefits to workers in all industries, since otherwise the profits in any particular business would depend on the success or failure of that special industry. Many laborers would then suffer for the mistakes of their overseers, while others might profit inequitably because of the skill of their leaders or the demands of the public. Indeed, they might even profit unjustly through the power of their monopoly by compelling consumers to pay high and unfair prices.

Industrial organization, therefore, must have a broad base as its foundation, such as the pioneer labor industrial establishments in Israel, so that the largest possible number of people may profit from their operations—both as consumers and producers. Such public corporations, not dependent solely upon the votes of shareholders, will also naturally strive to set a high standard of quality and a fair price, to which private industry will have to conform. It will always be the duty of the government to supervise such large aggregations of capital-labor corporations so that they shall operate for the benefit of the public as a whole; and, by holding the scales of even-handed justice, also permit private enterprise full and free competition—as in the classic case of state savings bank insurance in competition with other forms of life insurance.

The economy of the state of Israel is being built upon the solid foundation of a capital-labor relationship in which the all-inclusive class of consumers must prove to be the determining factor in economic life. Just as the cooperative farm settlements will operate to protect the workers against periods of unemployment, so the large aggregations of capital-labor corporations, based upon consumers' requirements, must operate in the evolution of an industrial democracy.

Many mistakes were made in the first few years after the establishment of the state of Israel in attempts of over-regulation, that sometimes seems to accompany a socialist labor government, in practice, even though not countenanced in socialist theory. There were too many "permits" and "licenses" which unnecessarily restricted private enterprise instead of permitting individual initiative to compete with the larger public corporations. At the same time, there was a failure to regulate large aggregations of capital funds, accumulated by insurance companies, which are under such rigid control in the United States.

For example, while an inflationary period was easily recognized, the large life insurance companies practically closed down their mortgage loans in Israel and, instead, invested their bulging assets in real estate equities, therefore adding to the speculative craze which feeds upon inflation. (In this respect, Israel was following light-heartedly the British practice which exercises little super-vision over insurance companies, as compared with American states.) And yet, this is precisely the field where a wise capitalist government must exercise its regulatory powers to the fullest extent. By virtually decreeing that life insurance companies must invest the major portion of their assets in mortgage loans and government bonds, the United States has been able to check, to a very large extent, inflationary tendencies and, at the same time, encourage building activities, offering extra employment and benefits to the public at large.

There is a distinct preference among the people of Israel to bear the burden of interest payments as against profits for industry or commerce. This may be the result of a hangover from Central European socialist doctrine, in which profits were stigmatized as the "unearned incre-ment" from a "surplus value" taken from labor—while interest was often regarded as an inevitable charge for the use of capital. The distinction has no real basis in eco-nomics, for interest may often prove as burdensome as profits, while the latter has the advantage of testing the competitive values of any industry. Undoubtedly, Israel has much to learn from American financial operations, where both interest and profits are coordinated in a system of common and preferred shares, as well as interest-bear-ing bonds and debentures. But for the present we must deal with a psychology which looks askance at profits as something almost illegal.

I recall an incident in the development of an early agri-cultural settlement, where I urged that the settlers must conserve and build up capital for the common good of this cooperative farm colony. At the mention of the word "capital," there was consternation among the group of settlers. "We want no 'capital,'" they said. I then began to explain that they must have tractors and other necessary agricultural machinery. "Oh! You mean 'mittl' (means)." As long as the hated word "capital" was not used among a people striving for a socialist brotherhood, they were perfectly satisfied. They needed "means" for improving their lot, but not "capital"!

There is every indication that this early reaction to capital and profits is now undergoing a profound change— largely as a result of the very competition between private and public enterprise. An illustration is the friendly co-operation between the Migdal Insurance Company, a privately owned joint stock company, and the "Hassneh," owned and directed by the Histadruth Labor Party, which is the largest in the country. By the interaction between business, organized on the basis of profits, and public activities founded for the benefit of the all-inclusive class of consumers, Israel will show the way toward an economic system that combines profitable management with deep concern for the public at large.

The lesson of America, with its large-scale business operations, proves the value of the profit motive as the necessary ingredient in the evolution of a better balanced economic system. The people of Israel are now becoming convinced that "profits" are not something taken away from the consumer, but rather a substantial proof that the gains for the consumer are even larger—as, for example, when a huge food chain, with its supermarkets, can operate successfully with a net profit of only one-half cent for every dollar of sales. The one-half of 1 per cent is more than "earned" by the entrepreneurs by careful management, as opposed to state ownership and control. Indeed, the average profits of large corporations are, on the whole, not more than would be required for interest payments for capital obtained by any public corporation.

The people of Israel are being prepared for this American message, as illustrated by the history of the excellent cooperative societies that control the extensive bus system that covers the country. Starting as small groups of bus drivers who were given franchises over limited roads, almost all of whom were members of the socialist (Histadruth) Party, but thriving even on a very moderate price charged, the membership in these cooperative bus groups became so valuable that the privilege of inheriting the membership—or selling for the benefit of a deceased member—was worth many thousands of dollars. This kind of "cooperative" profit was accepted with equanimity until the public began to demand price cuts or the alternative of state-operated buses. We then had the curious situation, several years ago, of the socialist-minded members of the cooperative bus societies resisting state ownership, while the "bourgeois" elements were vociferous in the demand for nationalization—that the state should own the means of transportation! The best solution was eventually adopted: regulation of these public utilities while they remained in the "private" control of these cooperatives. This is the kind of middle ground which, thanks to American example, is becoming the normal economic procedure in Israel.

America, indeed, has a lesson to teach the infant state of Israel in this respect that may prove salutory: state interference and economic controls are to be used sparingly and only when self-regulation, through the normal process of competition with the large public corporations, might become inoperative, in times of emergency and crisis. When this principle is incorporated in the framework of the commonwealth of Israel, with its labor cooperative settlements, and its principle of fostering public corporations for the benefit of consumers, an enlightened message of great value for economic freedom may ensue for the benefit of the whole world.

CHAPTER FIVE

Parliament and
Constitutional Government

In many respects, the new state of Israel is fortunate in that it can start from scratch, without political or legal commitments to any other state. It has all the past experience of mankind upon which to draw, limited only by the general principle of equality for "all the inhabitants of the Land" as provided in the Old Testament, and with the implicit injunction in its Declaration of Independence not to discriminate on the grounds of race, religion or nationality. This calls to mind the similar American Bill of Rights, constituting the first ten amendments to the United States Constitution, which protects the individual citizen against his own government, whether state or federal. Sooner, rather than later, Israel must have a written constitution, whereby every citizen and even "the stranger within the gates" will be safeguarded by an adequate and independent judicial system against any encroachment by the government or its officials.

I have no faith in what is known as a unwritten constitution. Our forefathers, who compiled the Talmud, after centuries of experience with what might be called

an unwritten constitution in the "oral law," later discovered that even the unwritten commentaries on the
Bible and the precepts of Hebrew Law were recorded in
the Mishnah, which preceded the Talmud. An unwritten
constitution like that of Great Britain, which may be
repudiated by a mere majority vote in Parliament, is a
delusion, pure but not so simple. People may be hood-
winked into the belief that there are certain inviolable
rights—such as "an Englishman's home is his castle"—
which may be a good dream picture, but when the crisis
comes and its is necessary to invoke such "natural rights"
of an Englishman, resort must be had to a "Ship Money"
case by a sturdy John Hampden. Even then, that case was
finally resolved not in a court of law—where Hampden
was defeated—but in the Cromwellian Revolution. The
American colonists' reliance upon an unwritten English
constitution finally resulted in the Revolutionary War,
which set these States free.

Any constitution that requires a successful war to establish its validity as a "higher law" is merely an invitation
to rebellion. It is true that even the United States had to
face a Civil War, but this was rather a War between the
States—always possible in a divided world—rather than a
struggle over civil rights. In any event, unlike successful
revolutions against an unwritten constitution, the federal
government of the United States, under President Lincoln,
was successful in preserving and upholding the written
Constitution.

Indeed, it was largely the failure of British officialdom
to understand the meaning and significance of a written
constitution that embroiled Great Britain in a policy of
repeated violations of the Palestine Mandate, which had

been clearly formulated by the League of Nations as the written and fundamental law of the Holy Land. All rules and regulations of the mandatory power were thereby necessarily subordinate to this charter. But the British Colonial Office assumed, from the very outset, that any decree issued from Downing Street, under some general parliamentary statute, was valid even though it might be clearly in opposition to the terms of the Mandate as the supreme law of the land. The Jews, and particularly those trained under American traditions of constitutional government, naturally assumed that any decree of a Palestine High Commissioner might be declared invalid by the Mandates Commission of the League of Nations, as the superior body from which Great Britain had received its authority as trustee for the establishment of the Jewish National Home.

This was in effect conceded by Malcolm MacDonald, as Colonial Secretary, when he appeared before the Mandates Commission in June, 1939, to defend the White Paper Policy, which restricted Jewish immigration and limited land purchases. In his presentation of the case, he told the Mandates Commission: "Of course you gentlemen have the last word." This was a plain intimation that if the Mandates Commission found the proposed restrictions under the White Paper "as not in consonance with the Mandate," such White Paper policy would be withdrawn as null and void, i.e., unconstitutional. The Mandates Commission of the League of Nations did so declare, yet the vicious practice of an unwritten constitution evidently prompted MacDonald to treat this international trust obligation of the Palestine Mandate as a mere earlier act of Parliament, subject to repeal by a later vote, despite

86

the illegality attached to such a procedure in the judicial opinion of the Mandates Commission.

Therefore, from the American point of view, the refugees coming into Palestine without British visas were not "illegal immigrants"—no matter how hard the British press and the government-controlled British Broadcasting Corporation tried to prove otherwise. Indeed, it was the decree of the British government barring immigrants from the Jewish National Home that was illegal—as vouched for by the highest authority, the Mandates Commission of the League of Nations. In the eyes of Americans, Jews and Gentiles alike, the White Paper itself, restricting immigration in spite of the vote of the Mandates Commission, was an illegal decree and therefore could not create illegal immigrants.

In short, with an unwritten constitution, mandatory trust obligations, treaty rights, even personal liberty and the principle of equality before the law are never safe, but always subject to a mere majority vote of a Parliament or legislature. According to this practice courts, both in Palestine and in England, repeatedly ruled that they were bound only by the laws and ordinances promulgated by the High Commissioner, even when such rules were plainly repugnant to the terms of the Palestine Mandate.

To protect the civil rights of the inhabitants of any state, there is no surer way than to enshrine a written constitution as a fundamental law, with an independent judiciary to enforce its injunctions, even to the extent, when necessary, of declaring null and void any legislation which the Supreme Court (of last resort) may decide is unconstitutional. This is the American practice, which over a century and a half has proven a true safeguard for

87

the liberty of the individual and the freedom of the nation. It is even more important in a small state like Israel, where the rights and privileges of an Arab minority, for example, would then be safeguarded by judicial process, instead of by resort to diplomatic representations of dangerous outside interference.

As to the contents of the written constitution, it must necessarily include provisions similar to the Bill of Rights, embodying the principles inherited from the French Revolution: "Equality, Liberty and Fraternity." While it is no longer fashionable to divide a government into three branches (as promulgated by Montesquieu), because the legislative and executive powers are naturally interrelated, yet the judiciary must at all times remain a branch independent of changing governmental machinery. That is the only way to preserve stability of institutions, while protecting the liberty of the individual. Accordingly Israel, following the American precedent, has a Supreme Court, with Justices appointed for life (or "during good behavior," to use the language of the Constitution of the United States), who should be subject only to removal for wrongdoing, in impeachment proceedings, by a two-thirds vote of the legislative body.

Fortunately, Israel has developed a judicial system with honest, fearless and learned judges, of which it may well be proud. In order to maintain this high standard, Israel must implement one further provision, namely, that the judges should be appointed by the President who is free from all party obligations, even though the Knesset (or Parliament) may have the right of confirmation.

The written constitution is always subject to amendment from time to time but, of course, with more safeguards than in the case of the enactment of an ordinary law. I would suggest that a constitutional majority of more than sixty votes (in a Knesset, membership of 120) should be required to recommend any amendment for adoption, which might then become part of the fundamental law when repassed by a constitutional two-thirds majority in the Knesset, after an appropriate interval for a cooling-off process. Yet, it must always be remembered that a constitution consists not only of the written words, but includes the successive judicial interpretations placed upon it from time to time. It shall be the devoted labors of a just and wise judiciary that must safeguard the heritage of the Children of Israel and infuse the old spirit of the ancient prophets in the written constitution of the new state of Israel.

The membership in the Knesset as the legislative body in the state of Israel has been fixed at 120. This is a good number, sufficient for debate, and yet not unwieldy as a lawmaking body. But the adoption of the principle of proportional representation in the election of its membership has led to a serious debate on the whole question of single constituencies versus party tickets. Whatever may be the merits of either system, the first election in the state of Israel on January 25, 1949 (later confirmed by the experience in the election in the summer of 1951) demonstrated conclusively that the system of proportional representation, with candidates proposed by each political party, is more suitable to this small country and its population, with its ingrained emphasis on ideology. Not a single individual, no matter how important his name, standing alone as a candidate for the legislative assembly, received enough votes to qualify for membership; parties

89

standing for definite and clearly announced programs, from the Socialists on the left to the religious groups on the right, secured the largest numbers of members.

It is clear that in the future, political affiliations in the state of Israel will follow rather the continental European system of party groups in its legislative assembly, in preference to the Anglo-Saxon practice of single constituencies (for a Parliament or a Congress), which tends to encourage a two-party system of government. The latter system, based upon the election of candidates by pluralities, in single constituencies, which tends to foster an administration party and its counterpart, the loyal opposition, seems peculiarly fitted for a population trained in the tradition of the mother of parliaments. But most Europeans, striving toward a democratic form of government, tend to divide along ideological lines and principles, and most of the Jewish immigrants into Israel seem to have been influenced in that way of political life.

Yet, there is no valid reason why the state of Israel should become a prey to the vicious party system of Central Europe where as in France, for example, the government was constantly at sea, with one Cabinet after another thrown overboard in a seesaw of party politics, which makes stable government impossible. This is less the fault of any system of proportional representation than the failure to apply well-tested political practices that have been developed in the United States of America. In the latter country, when a Congress is elected for two years, it *stays put*, and is not subject to dissolution by the threat of any Cabinet resignation, as in Great Britain. It simply must legislate for the country, together with the coordinate branch, the United States Senate, and administer the government, together with the executive power of the President which is beyond its reach (except in the unusual circumstances of impeachment proceedings).

The constitution of Israel should, therefore, make provision, similarly, for a stable executive through the election by the Knesset of the executive power (including the Prime Minister and his Cabinet) for a *definite period* (just as in America, the President is elected for a definite term), instead of following the usual European practice, wherein the executive power is subject to changing majorities within the Legislative Chamber—often at the whim of a few recalcitrant party leaders.

Accordingly, the Prime Minister should be selected by the Knesset for a definite period of two years and charged with the duty of constituting a cabinet for the conduct of his administration; but no Prime Minister or Cabinet might be removed during the term of office, *except upon a two-thirds vote of the Knesset,* after charges leading to impeachment proceedings. This would effectively eliminate unhealthy partisan politics, so reminiscent of the unstable governments of Central Europe. In effect, the Knesset would simply establish an executive or governing body, known as the Cabinet, for a relatively short period of two years. This committee, headed by the Prime Minister, would not be disturbed during its term of office, except in case of wrongdoing calling for impeachment.

This would at the same time do away with the evils of snap elections, such as often determine the dissolution of a British Parliament—for example, the false issue of a "hang the Kaiser" campaign after World War I, resulting in the return of a large conservative majority which, instead of hanging the Kaiser, soon turned out of office

Prime Minister David Lloyd George who led the victorious war effort. The English practice which allows the Prime Minister of Great Britain to choose the time and occasion for the election of a Parliament, within the five-year period, sometimes reduces the legislative power to a mere shadow in the hands of shrewd but unprincipaled politicians. On the contrary, the Prime Minister, chosen by the lawmaking body, should have a certain amount of freedom which would be reviewed every two years.

Finally, the real success or failure of any government must rest upon the representatives of the people in the lawmaking assembly. Under the multiple party system, chosen by proportional representation, it is doubly important not only that the executive power be firmly established for a definite term, but also that the chosen representatives of the people should feel themselves responsible primarily to the people as a whole rather than to any party boss or Prime Minister. This can be safeguarded by elevating membership in the Knesset to a position of high honor, not to be so lightly thrown away in any snap election, often subject to manipulation by some politician for mere party gains.

On the other hand, the practice of allowing a Prime Minister and his Cabinet to decide when to call for an election, often enables the party in power to choose the time and issue upon which to "go to the country" instead of allowing the electorate to select its representatives on the basis of the record of the administration as a whole. The issue over the false Zinoviev letter, for example, which virtually decided the crucial British Parliamentary election of October, 1924, was a particularly vicious practice of a "red herring" drawn into a political campaign—even though in this case the election turned against the party in power. It is much wiser to provide, by law, a definite election date for members of the Knesset so that voters may look forward to a review of the whole record of the Prime Minister and his Cabinet.

The day set for the selection of members of the Knesset might very well be the last Saturday night (and succeeding day) in November, every odd-numbered year, in commemoration of the vote in the United Nations Assembly, which gave international sanction to the creation of the Jewish state on November 29, 1947. The same day of every even-numbered year might be set aside for the election of members to the municipal councils, of which one-half should be elected biannually, to hold office for a period of four years.

Finally, America has something to offer along this line, even though its government is based upon the two-party system. While the members of the House of Representatives, or lower House, are elected for a definite period of two years, and the President for a four-year term, the United States Senate constitutes a *permanent* body, only one-third of its membership being elected biannually, with each Senator holding office for six years. The Senate, with its tradition of *continuity*, shares with the President the determination of foreign policy and reflects the major changes in national life. It can play this important role all the better because, as a permanent body with only one-third of its personnel changed every two years, it offers the prospect of stability which cannot be supplied by a chamber often composed—if not decomposed—by every gust of party passion.

Accordingly, since Israel is committed to the principle of proportional representation, it seems highly desirable that the Knesset (its Parliament of a single house) be constituted as a permanent body with only one-half of its membership chosen every two years, each member holding office for a period of four years, in order to preserve the continuity of this one lawmaking body. This would constitute the Knesset as a permanent governmental force which would rule the state through its selection of the Prime Minister and his Cabinet for definite terms of two years (subject only to removal by impeachment, for some grave offense).

Following this plan, sixty members would be elected to the Knesset every other year, after first dividing the present membership into two classes, one retiring two years after election and the second after a four year period. Thereafter, all members would be elected for a definite period of four years every second year. At the same time, it would be highly advisable, as a wise compromise between single constituencies and party lists, to divide the territory of Israel into three permanent electoral districts, with Galilee, the Sharon Plain and the South (including the Negev) so divided that after each census these districts of approximately equal population, with Haifa, Tel Aviv and Jerusalem as their respective centers, shall each elect twenty members every second year as its quota of representatives in the Knesset. This would inevitably reduce the prospect of party splinters, for the major political groups would almost certainly divide the twenty successful candidates in each district among themselves.

Such a system of election by large districts seems to me highly preferable to single constituencies (inherent in the two-party system of government) where party slogans hold strong away, so that one constituency may persist in electing a particular local representative to Parliament or Congress, who is hardly a credit to the nation or his state.

who desires to ride on the Jewish holiday must either use his private car or take a taxi, for the state naturally will not discriminate against those who do not use public conveyances. Likewise, the army uses only Kosher food and its influence is immense, since the example set by a regular standing army permeates the whole economy—yet there is no attempt to restrict the diet in restaurants or private homes.

Many of those who complain about "irreligion" in Israel may, indeed, miss some favorite dishes because non-Kosher food is sometimes difficult to obtain! It is perhaps not too much to say that for every devout Jew in America there are, in proportion to the population, at least ten in the same category in Israel. The oft-repeated current criticism is simply the reflection of a natural desire for the Jewish Israeli to be better than ourselves, representing the place where a great religious heritage must be preserved.

But we are often confronted with the opposite criticism: that the state of Israel tends to operate as a theocracy, opposing the modern concepts of liberal world opinion. Nothing could be further from the truth. How well Israel has performed the arduous duty of steering the ship of state between the Scylla and Charybdis or religious nonconformity and the regimentation of a theocracy is best illustrated by the perfect toleration accorded not only to all Jewish religious sects, but to the different Christian churches and Moslems as well.

Naturally, the impress of the Old Testament lies strongly upon the land and its institutions, but this is the result rather of the morals derived from the Bible and the prevailing laws and civilization which grew out of its centuries of influence. Thus, the United States Supreme

Yet such a representative may wield great influence, out of all proportion to his abilities, when especially, under the rules of seniority, he may become the chairman of an important committee. Thus, in Republican administrations some local constituency in Maine or the Middle West often may wield extraordinary influence out of all proportion to its population and importance, even against the general public interest. Equally, in a Democratic administration, some Senator from South Carolina or Mississippi may exercise powers for which the voters of New York or Massachusetts are held responsible.

On the other hand, by a system of proportional representation, with lists from each party covering relatively large districts, as outlined above, we are fairly certain to secure the leadership of the most prominent men, representative of the country as a whole, instead of some special restricted district.

There is one substantial advantage that a parliamentary government such as Israel has over constitutional government, where the executive power is lodged in a single individual. In the former, the Prime Minister must face the opinions and arguments of the other responsible Cabinet members and the decision is usually the majority opinion, even when the Prime Minister is an exceptionally able leader. In that case, he is powerful enough to persuade the others to his point of view. But in the constitutional form of government the President, especially in foreign affairs, can, and does, often commit the country against the majority of his own Cabinet.

So far America has been particularly fortunate and, in the great crisis of the Civil War, Lincoln saved the Union where the Cabinet might have hesitated. Yet the crisis brought on particularly by an illness of a President may be a source of real danger to the country. So far we have been spared the disaster from a demented dictator like Hitler or a monomaniac like Stalin but the gradual, and sometimes imperceptible, degeneration of even a great mind in the presidential office must enjoin us to make constitutional provision against such an occurrence. In Democratic Israel, it is the Prime Minister and his Cabinet that make the policies. Thus such a danger is completely obviated.

The President is chosen by the Knesset for a five-year period and likewise his successor (due to death, resignation or vacancy in that office). The President symbolizes the sovereignty of the state, and also upon him would rest the duty of designating the members of the judiciary, with life tenure (subject to the approval of the Knesset), as a third independent force in the state. The actual government administration would, of course, rest with the Prime Minister and his Cabinet who, with the President, would constitute the government of the state.

Under such a clarified political system, the economy of the state of Israel would rest securely upon a threefold solid foundation of cooperative farming settlements (for the elimination of unemployment), public control of natural resources (including rent income from increasing land values), and development of public corporations for the benefit of consumers, in equal competition with private industry and individual initiative. The evolution of such a program should prove a message of worldwide significance, from which humanity might achieve the prospect of a regime of social justice based upon individual liberty.

CHAPTER SIX

Church and State in Israel

American tourists returning from Israel sometimes profess to be disturbed by the secular attitude on the part of a large segment of the Israeli population. They complain that a large number seem to be uninfluenced by the profound impact that Judaism should have upon the Jewish state. In short, such visitors would prefer a closer affiliation between the Israeli state and Judaism as a religion.

Despite the fact that such critics are seldom the adherents of a strict orthodoxy, they are likely to demand strict religious observance on the part of the membership of some isolated collective farm settlement. Such tourists often point to the laxity in observance of the Sabbath on the part of many Israelis, altogether oblivious to the fact that, in proportion to the population, the performance of Jewish rites are far more general in Israel than anywhere else in the world—America included. This, of course, is perfectly natural for the entire milieu in Israel lends itself to the encouragement of Jewish religious practices. Thus, neither the railways nor the buses operate on the Sabbath (except for a solitary service to Mt. Carmel). The citizen

Court, for example, has correctly ruled that America is a Christian country (correctly bearing in mind the whole complex of its civilization) and just so is the state of Israel a Jewish country, yet with religious freedom for all the inhabitants thereof.

There can be no denial of the tremendous impact of the Hebrew Bible upon the cultural life of Israel, where nearly every hill and vale is a reminder of some passage in the Holy Scriptures. Indeed, the very geography of Israel is a living commentary upon the long stretch of Jewish history, and its influence permeates the laws and customs of the whole population. To attempt to separate the people of Israel from the results of Jewish history or the influence of Judaism is a task well nigh impossible. The great majority of the Israeli population is an amalgam of the national characteristics and Jewish religious practices of a long-suffering people, so intertwined as almost to compose elements in a remarkable chemical compound. The Moslem and Christian minority share a common country with the Jewish majority in which Judaism, as a mother religion, is necessarily reflected in the thoughts and aspirations of the people as a whole. With no established Church and with full religious freedom for all, based upon traditions of liberty that go back for centuries, little Israel will stand by the side of large America in the long struggle for liberty of conscience and freedom of thought and its expression.

Perhaps a distinction should be made between the positive and negative obligations under the heading of religion. Some years ago the Israel Supreme Court disallowed polygamy, despite the objection raised by a Mohammedan defendant that his religion permits him to take more than

99

one wife (since four are allowed in the Koran). The Court correctly ruled that there was no religious obligation upon an Arab to take four wives, but only a *permission,* which need not be exercised in a modern state like Israel, where polygamy is outlawed. And so, following a similar precedent, while neither in dietary laws nor in Sabbath observance does the state prescribe any positive rules binding the individual, yet the immemorial practices of Judaism are inevitably reflected in the public services of the state of Israel.

To those who fear that Judaism as a religion may be weakened in the secular state of Israel, America stands as the best example of a country in which there is increased religious observance under a secular legal system. But perhaps an old story that I heard in Israel—almost reminiscent of the famous parables of the New Testament—will best express the relation of the Jew to the state of Israel. The story goes that the sainted Rabbi Kook, of Jerusalem, visiting a Kvutzah farm settlement, was surprised to learn that the dietary laws were not being observed and that even on the Sabbath the members of this cooperative used their horses not, it is true, for work, but for sport. When the Rabbi tried gently to reprimand the group, they replied that in this modern age it was no longer important to observe the old regulations, and that they were doing their duty by redeeming the soil and planting orange groves.

Whereupon Rabbi Kook answered with a fable that "once upon a time," before World War I, when the Turkish Sultan ruled in Palestine, a rumor ran through the land that the old Wailing Wall, the site and only reminder of the ancient Holy Temple, was about to be sold at public auction. There was a natural concern lest it fall into the hands of a non-Jew, who might desecrate and destroy this old memorial. And so, when the date for the auction arrived, many Jews appeared at the site, with fear and trembling, and watched the bidders contest for the possession of this ancient holy ruin. At last it was knocked down to one whom they recognized as a Jew, and so they approached him with gladness in their hearts, and asked what he proposed to do with this famous memorial of the past. "Do," said he, "I have no use for such old ruins. I shall clear the ground and plant a modern orange grove." The members of the Kvutzah listened intently and then, with one voice, cried, "Rabbi, even we wouldn't let him do it."

All the people in Israel may not follow religiously every rule and regulation of Judaism, but inevitably they form the living bridge between the past and the future—and to their devoted hands may be left the development of modern Judaism.

CHAPTER SEVEN

The Wandering Jew
and the Law of the Return

Immigration has always been the crux of the Palestine problem—the key that has opened the door to the House of Israel. The failure of the British government to recognize this simple truth muddied the living waters of Jewish Palestine for a whole generation, from the Balfour Declaration of 1917 until the S.S. *Exodus* carried its unfortunate human freight back from the shores of Palestine to Hamburg, Germany, in the summer of 1947—and then once more to Cyprus, whence these refugees might almost look upon the shores of Israel, but might not enter the land of their forefathers. Why the British should have failed to recognize the inevitable connection between Palestine and Jewish immigration is difficult to understand, for not only Balfour but also Lloyd George, as Prime Minister, regarded Palestine as the major contribution of World War I to solving the problem of "Jewish homelessness."

While Winston Churchill was Colonial Secretary in 1922, the Zionist organization presumably surrendered its right to the territory of Trans-Jordan, which was included under the proposed Palestine mandate, in exchange for the promise of practically free immigration into the territory west of the Jordan, based only upon the formula of *economic absorptive capacity.* Soon thereafter, his successor in the British Colonial Office launched upon a program of restricting Jewish immigration to a point "never contemplated" in the Balfour Declaration and the Palestine mandate, as both Lloyd George and Winston Churchill later testified. Such a policy might have led to a Palestine solution which would reduce the Jews to the status of a hopeless minority (under British protection). For an imperialistic program, the presence of such a British-protected Jewish minority in Palestine would have proven a godsend, for it offered Britain the opportunity, on the plea of humanity, to interfere continually in Palestine and stay in the country indefinitely. Indeed, this policy, however unjustified, might have succeeded, despite the protests of the Zionist organization, but for the explosive pressure of Jewish immigration.

The problem of immigration for the "wandering Jew" has been a permanent fixture during most of the last nineteen centuries. Indeed, it was only in the half century between the infamous May Laws (under the Czar) of 1881, up to 1924, that Jews, for the first time in their long history, were free to move in large numbers from centers of persecution. The Zionist organization, gradually assuming the role of a trustee over Jewish interests during that period, was greatly concerned lest the doors of Palestine be closed in the days of the dire calamity of European Jewry.

In the spring of 1939, or six months before Hitler's attack on Poland, the public press was filled with heartrending accounts of the plight of 907 Jewish refugees huddled together on the S.S. *St. Louis,* shuttled back and forth upon the wide waters of the Atlantic, after admission was denied them in Cuba on the ground that their visas were not in order. Germany had forced them into exile, but even the great democracies were loath to make an exception and offer to make a place of refuge for less than one thousand poor souls who, after being forced out of Europe, were sustained in the hope that the visas for which they had paid fabulous sums were good and valid. The debate was long and statesmanlike, while the S.S. *St. Louis* went back and forth with its human cargo. Finally, through the superhuman efforts of Jewish relief organizations, we were fortunate in allotting these poor victims of Nazi persecution among the four western democracies of England, France, Belgium and Holland. We must remember that it took the combined powers of mercy of two world empires, aided by the generous help of two smaller nations in Europe, to take care of 907 Jews —a symbol that we were even then living in a closed world, and a true harbinger of the stress and strain that heralded World War II.

The New York Times of June 14, 1939, reported that the British Undersecretary of the Home Office explained that even this generosity was due to the exceptional circumstances resulting from "the fact that all these people had been granted visas which later were not honored." This high British official went on to state that: "It is of the first importance that the arrangements for immigration of Jewish refugees from Germany shall proceed in accordance with an orderly program, and that no encouragement shall be given to any idea that refugees may leave Germany before arrangements have been completed for their reception." The matter of "first importance," let it be noted, was not the saving of refugees, but the denial of visas!

On the basis of past history, we may hope for the best of all possible worlds, but common sense warned us not to expect much better terms for the wandering Jews after the war. It is our bounden duty to our children and our children's children to find a haven of refuge where a Jew may enter "as of right, and not on sufferance."

For a moment, consider now the plight of some 907 Irish Catholic refugees fleeing from London, whence they might have been expelled for membership in the Irish Volunteer Army. I am not assuming that the doors of Ellis Island would have been opened to them, although speeches in their favor might have been heard in the halls of Congress and Parliament. I am not supposing that Belgium, Holland and France would have opened their doors more willingly than to the refugee Jews, or without a stern warning from some high official in the British Empire. I am simply asserting the fact that in the case of some 907 Londoners of the Irish Catholic "persuasion," traveling in a ship across the Atlantic, even after they had been denied admittance, the little Irish Free State, poor and partitioned, would have gladly opened its doors and claimed them as her sons and her daughters. That is the essence of the quest for a Jewish commonwealth—not any metaphysical argument over nationalism, or any theoretical dispute over race and religion, but the world challenge: "To be or not to be, that is the question."

It was, therefore, only natural to assume that the most important element in the Balfour Declaration in 1917 was the right of Jews freely to immigrate to the old land of their forefathers. That the Jews would never peacefully surrender such a right, derived legally from the Balfour Declaration and the Palestine mandate, and morally from the historic connection with the land of the Bible, should have been clear to any statesman. It was the glaring failure to recognize this simple fact which led Great Britain into the impasse, culminating, in 1939, when the British Colonial Office limited Jewish immigration into Palestine to fifteen thousand immigrants a year, during a five-year period, with the further proviso that no further immigration whatsoever would be permitted, except with "Arab consent"—which the British government must have known full well would not be forthcoming.

Winston Churchill, speaking in the House of Commons, called this new policy "plainly the breach and repudiation of the Balfour Declaration, the provision that Jewish immigration can be stopped in five years' time by a decision of an Arab majority." He went on to state that "long before these five years are past, however, there will be a Britain which knows how to keep its word on the Balfour Declaration, and is not afraid to do so, or believe me, we shall find ourselves relieved of many overseas responsibilities other than those comprised within the Palestine mandate."

These prophetic words were uttered almost on the eve of World War II which, in its aftermath, brought the loss of immense British colonial possessions, including India, so that Churchill's pronouncement might be viewed as a punishment visited upon Great Britain for failure to honor its Palestine obligations. Later, as Prime Minister, he was to add that he was not chosen as His Majesty's First Minister in order "to preside over the liquidation of the British

Empire," but he clearly foresaw the inevitable trend that began with the repudiation of obligations under the Palestine mandate, in 1939, and continued with the scuttling policy of Ernest Bevin, as indicated later, when he turned over the whole Palestine problem to the United Nations.

The policy of restricting Jewish immigration into Palestine came at a most inopportune time—just when the need was greatest—preceding Hitler's war against civilization, when some at least of the six million innocent Jewish victims might otherwise have found a haven of refuge in the future state of Israel. So the Jews of Palestine went into World War II as the ally of Great Britain, but with a heavy heart, remembering the injunction of Ben-Gurion (later to become the first Prime Minister of Israel) that "We shall fight the war as if there were no White Paper (restricting immigration), and we shall fight the White Paper as if there is no war."

But when the world war was ended, and the British Labor Party came into power in the summer of 1945, pledged to the policy of opening the gates of Palestine to Jewish immigration, Jews the world over had high hopes that the old policy of restriction would speedily be swept away.

Unfortunately, just at this juncture, came the fateful intervention of Ernest Bevin as the new Foreign Minister. Bevin proceeded to nullify the solemn pledges made by the Labor Party in its pre-election campaign. It was largely his intransigent attitude that made it clear to all that only the building of a Jewish state would solve the problem of Jewish immigration. In a true sense, therefore, it may be well said that Bevin, more than any other single individual, is responsible for the creation of the state of Israel!

We are apt to overlook the historic fact that the great century of free immigration into the United States, which ended with the restrictive policy of 1924, was exceptional in every respect both in time and space. Never before in history were large masses of men able to move freely, without war, from country to country. And even in this golden epoch of free immigration, large and attractive areas like South Africa and Australia were bound to policies of restriction in immigration as a prelude to the "closed world" in which we are living today. Needless to say, South Africa is paying a heavy price for this ostrich-like policy; now less than three million whites are living midst a volcano of over nine million of the colored race. Australia was saved from Japanese conquest by the grace of America, which herself was made so strong by a century of immigration that she can now afford the luxury of a limited closed-door policy.

But, if every segment of humanity be provided with a minimum space as a haven of refuge to which its members may repair, there is some hope also for a closed door against human strife over mere living space. That is the lesson of Israel in the contracted and restrictive world of today. The enactment by the Israeli Parliament of the "Law of the Return" highlights the sacred principle of a right to living space for any sector of humanity. For centuries the wandering Jew has been forced to knock at closed doors which, at best, were grudgingly and only partly opened by some ruling prince, bent upon admitting only just enough Jews necessary for the economic well-being of his province. Seldom if ever was any consideration given to the requirements of the hunted Jew himself, shuttling back and forth over the face of the continent of Europe and the Mediterranean basin. But now, at least as long as the state of Israel shall exist, whenever and wherever the Jew is persecuted and discriminated against on the grounds of race or religion, there will always be an open door through which he may pass to a place of refuge in the land of Israel.

The historic law of a right to return should be enshrined in the hearts of all humanity. No man should be kept as a prisoner in any country, and every human being should have at least one free land to which he might turn in the dark days of persecution and discrimination. All humanity may well profit from this sound doctrine of the "Law of the Return," so graphically described by Prime Minister Ben-Gurion when he sponsored "the incomparably historic occasion wherein it was approved and signed by every party in the House" (the Knesset).

As a matter of historic fact, the pressure for Jewish immigration was the primary cause in the establishment of the Jewish state, since Arab opposition to free Jewish immigration into Palestine made it impossible for any fair compromise before Israel's War of Independence. The Arabs of Palestine naturally feared that the continual flow of Jewish immigrants might soon reduce them to a minority in their own land (even though equal democratic treatment was assured to such a minority). No people can be expected peacefully to consent to be outnumbered on their own soil, and the attempts of the Ihud organization for a binational state—led by the revered figure of Dr. Judah L. Magnes of the Hebrew University—was therefore doomed to failure. Binationalism necessarily implied consent on the part of the Arab majority to agree to a formula of unrestricted Jewish immigration (or at least an immigration based on the principle of "economic absorptive capacity," which, in itself, would be a matter of serious dispute). This is something to which the Arabs would never consent. Indeed, the subject of Jewish immigration was the "irrepressible conflict" which unfortunately could be resolved—as it was—only by war.

Just as the southern states, before the Civil War, could not agree to permit any restrictions to the spread of slavery, because such restrictions meant ultimate death to their "peculiar institution"—no matter how reasonable it would appear to the people of the northern states— even so was unrestricted Jewish immigration anathema to the Arabs. On the other hand, the Jews could not accept restriction of Jewish immigration because this necessarily would result in reducing them to a hopeless minority, subject to the dictates of an Arab majority in the old land of Israel, while the crucial problem of Jewish homelessness would remain unsolved.

Only now when there is a Jewish state *de facto* and *de jure*, can we correctly envisage the problem of rapprochement, between the sovereign Jewish state and the Arab counterpart of Jordan. And a true solution will come, if at all, not through politics, but by an economic union, freely entered into between the two parts of ancient Palestine. This seems a distant prospect at the present time, but economic necessity may finally lead to a peace of fruitful cooperation between Arab and Jew.

The Jews have tried to build a common mixed state of Arabs and Jews—and failed. It matters not whether the failure be attributed to themselves, the Arabs, or the mandatory power. Destiny seems to decree that they shall stand apart—not as a chosen people, in any sense of superiority over others, but certainly as a "saving remnant" that has a message for the world. Reform Judaism, with its historic idea of a message, was correct, and only its geography was wrong. The message will come from Galilee and Judea in the old land of Israel, and not from Berlin or Hamburg. That message is being formulated day by day, in the Kvutzah settlements, in Galilee, and the Sharon Valley: the humanitarian message of cooperation in labor and communal living, on a purely voluntary basis, while preserving the democratic ideal of individual liberty.

When our forefathers came to rebuild the Second Temple, they had a Samaritan problem to deal with which was at least as serious as the Arab problem of today. But Ezra refused to compromise, preferring to divide Palestine into two parts, leaving Samaria (even as now) without the scope of the tiny Jewish state under Persian protection, so that he might be able to preserve that "saving remnant" of a compact Jewish nation. It was this second Hebrew commonwealth which later gave us the Maccabees and the Talmud, and introduced Christianity to a frustrated Roman Empire, thus preparing the way for a renaissance in barbarian Europe.

Today Ezra's choice was made, not by us, but for us, by Great Britain as the overlord of Palestine, and by the opposition of the Arabs. Ezra and his followers have sometimes been accused of a clannishness unworthy of the seers of the Old Testament. But the Talmud makes it clear that the phrase "chosen people" does not imply any assumption of superiority, but rather one of dedication—"Ye shall be a kingdom of Priests."

The legend of the argument between Moses and Israelites at the foot of Mount Sinai best illustrates the meaning of the "chosen people." The story goes that, when Moses told his followers that they were about to receive the Ten Commandments, to be faithfully observed in the name of the Lord of Israel, the people at first refused to accept these limitations upon their freedom of action—which they regarded as new shackles for ex-slaves. Only when Moses assured them that they really had no choice, for otherwise their angry God would bury them under Mount Sinai, were they resigned to the "burden of the law." (Our sensible ancestors preferred to live under "the burden" of the law rather than to die under Mount Sinai.) And so the Israelites became the "chosen people" because, as we are assured in the same legend, no other people could be found ready and willing to accept the onerous gifts of the Ten Commandments.

No wonder some skeptical Jew, looking back over a history of two thousand years of racial and religious discrimination, has uttered the prayer: "O Lord, we who are your chosen people, have suffered so long and so grievously, we pray you, choose another people, at least for some little time, until we shall have grown strong enough to bear our persecutions." The chosen people were dedicated to carry the heavy burden of the Law, whether they willed it or not—chosen to mitigate the trials and tribulations of a suffering humanity.

CHAPTER EIGHT

Immigrants and Refugee Capital

There is a collateral principle to the "Law of the Return," to which insufficient attention has been paid in the first decade during which the state of Israel was established. It is to be hoped that this may soon be remedied by appropriate legislation. "You take my life when you do take the means whereby I live," was the cry that Shakespeare put into the mouth of Shylock, ringing with all the ancient sorrows and pains of the wandering Jew. There must be also a place for refugee capital—in a world still frequently divided by discriminatory taxes and class-favored tariffs. We need only recall how many hundreds of millions of dollars were confiscated from Jewish businessmen by the Nazis, even in the years preceding World War II, to appreciate what this river of gold might have meant to the starved economy of Palestine in those days.

But capital is proverbially timid and requires more than verbal support and encouragement through "investment centers." Above all, it demands the creation of a spirit of confidence which "though thin as air, is strong as iron bands." Such confidence must be based, first of all, upon a stable currency, so that the investor may feel that the principal will be first secured by a sound currency, and that any possible profits that may come his way will not be reduced to unredeemable pounds in a depreciated international market. It was the fixed policy of the standard gold franc that made Switzerland the refuge for capital in the past, thereby paying handsome dividends to a prosperous and happy people. Of course, rich America or Canada, despite the strong inflationary tendency of recent years, can more easily control their currency, but this is largely the result of faith in their credit position, built up in the preceding century, even when America was a heavy debtor to Europe. The same policy of a stable currency has paid well in smaller states like Venezuela and Uruguay where refugee capital has done marvels in helping to develop the land.

Unfortunately, the problem of currency stabilization was but little understood in the first full flush of economic development in the new state of Israel; and yet nothing is more important to its future well-being. History has proven that every political revolution begins with the debauchery of the currency, so significantly illustrated in the French and Russian Revolutions—for as the monetary value diminishes from day to day, people instinctively feel that they are cheated and are bound to place the blame upon the government.

This is precisely where American experience may prove of supreme importance. In the early days of the American Republic, when Alexander Hamilton served as the first Secretary of the Treasury, he foresaw the significance of a sound currency. Despite strenuous opposition from those who could not understand why it was necessary to redeem "continental" obligations at full par value, thereby pouring wealth into the pockets of speculators and gamblers who were buying up such obligations for a few cents on the dollar, Hamilton insisted that the credit of the new government could be preserved only by honoring its commitments. The great Hamilton understood that the savings in interest rates alone for the future government debts would be worth many times the value of such a policy of redemption. He even lobbied in Congress, offering to place the capital of the United States toward the South, in its present location at Washington, in order to procure enough southern support which, with mercantile interests of the North, succeeded in establishing the "full faith and credit" of the government. By such measures the credit and, therefore, the currency of the infant United States was placed on a solid basis.

How much the credit of the state of Israel might have profited from such a lesson! But during its organization in May, 1948, there was no Jewish Hamilton who might have succeeded in establishing a sound currency as the *sine qua non* of its very existence. The state had to learn the hard way, by trial and error, the facts of economic life.

And yet, the state of Israel is peculiarly fitted by circumstances to protect its currency through the income of the various Zionist and Jewish institutions, which bring in a hundred million dollars or more annually in gifts. Such donations, received by the Jewish Agency from the United Jewish Appeal, the Jewish National Fund and other organizations, must be so channelized as to constitute a prior charge for the protection of Israel currency. No matter how pressing the need for construction or development or even the absorption of immigrants, the safeguarding of the currency represents a priority of the first order, which dare not be ignored. It may even be necessary to keep a substantially larger part of such donations as a regulatory fund, invested in liquid securities in London or New York, as a guarantee of stabilization in terms of pounds sterling or American dollars. Only after the Israel currency shall have been fully protected can there be effective plans for constructive development. Otherwise, all proposed schemes are built on sand, for the simple reason that private capital will not be interested on the basis of a profit return upon the shifting monetary values in international exchange.

Nor can government participation in development programs take the place of private investors, for government itself inevitably depends upon taxes and loans, while foreign currency available from bond issues becomes increasingly difficult to secure in a situation where the currency is unstable. In short, currency stabilization is the key to the economic well-being of the state of Israel. Once that is well established, we may proceed with the investment of such donated funds for internal constructive development as well as promote the immigration of individuals who, with their private means, will further benefit the state and its economy.

An additional support for the currency would be the land holdings of the Jewish National Fund, organized half a century ago for the purpose of acquiring land in Palestine as the inalienable property of the Jewish people—land which may be leased to individuals or groups, but never sold. It is necessary only to expand this principle for the Jewish National Fund gradually to acquire the more valuable urban lands in order to secure a solid backing for the currency. Such ground rents, usually increasing in value from year to year in an expanding economy, built upon immigration, will afford an assurance and protection no less certain than the gold buried in Fort Knox to safeguard the American dollar.

The question of currency stabilization and international monetary exchange is not a problem solely for the state of Israel but rather a matter of grave concern to the world at large. In this connection, the experience of the small state of Israel from its very inception might serve as an object lesson in the plans of the United Nations for a better world. When, by the action of Foreign Secretary Ernest Bevin, the Palestine pound was so unceremoniously "kicked out" of the sterling bloc on February 22, 1948, causing the infant state of Israel much suffering, it brought sharply to world attention a matter of grave import to all nations.

World economy has suffered immeasureably from the lack of a stable currency for international exchange. The dollar is now king everywhere except, of course, in the United States itself where, until recently, it was the subject matter of constant debate because of the threat of a runaway inflation. The Marshall Plan and successor plans have given some respite to countries receiving such aid, and may be helpful for a longer period, unless and until such extended aid may endanger the American economy. It is the mere *fear* that one cannot obtain dollars for pounds sterling or French francs on demand, at a reasonable and constant rate, that may lead to a world economic collapse. And yet we have the means at our disposal finally to remedy this situation, if only we recognize that there "is nothing to fear but fear itself."

117

What is the value of an International Monetary Fund if it is not to be employed as a stabilizing factor for world currency? Next only to a threat of world war comes the fear of currency depreciation, which so often leads to revolution in any country exposed to that danger. And yet, the remedy is at hand through control of the gold resources of Great Britain and the United States, even should others refuse to join the dollar-sterling bloc. The United States is not only the greatest creditor of England and France, but also the highest contributor, through the Marshall Plan and foreign aid, to a safe and sane world economy. Why not insist, through the United Nations, that the International Monetary Fund arrange that the pound, dollar, franc and German mark be placed on a firm and sound basis, interchangeable in the world market, as a primary condition for any further credits or economic aid?

All these countries have tremendous earning power, which is the true and firm foundation of all financial strength; and the natural resources of Canada and South Africa may bear some comparison to that of the United States, while the thrifty French peasant and the industrial might of a recovered Germany should be sufficient to secure ample support for such a financial bloc. But the very question of the mobilization of natural resources depends, to a very large extent, on currency stabilization which, in turn, should be the primary concern of the United Nations and the International Monetary Fund.

There is nothing to prevent a simultaneous deposit of gold and other commodities with the International Monetary Fund by Great Britain, France, Germany and the United States. Dollars, francs, marks and pounds sterling

118

would then be freely exchangeable at a fixed price on the international market, perhaps establishing the value of a pound sterling equivalent to 1,200 francs and also equivalent to $3.00 in United States currency. Every country in the world would be compelled, sooner rather than later, to make a compact with the United Nations so as to place its national currency upon the dollar-pound-franc basis, since otherwise it would be unable to trade in the international market. The United Nations would inevitably become even more important as an international organization, essential to the very life of every state and nation. It is by concentrating on various material interests like currency stabilization that the United Nations will grow stronger with the passing years.

Next to a stable currency for the state of Israel, we need a free economy if we are to attract refugee capital. By that we do not mean the absence of all government interference in business, but rather its reduction to a minimum. We can afford to allow enterprising leaders in industry the larger reward which their ingenuity may bring, for thereby we preserve incentive for constant improvement in industrial life, with the consequent increase in the economic surplus for the benefit of the nation as a whole.

Only in such a way can we attract the refugee capital so necessary in the upbuilding and development of the state of Israel. Indeed, in order to promote and safeguard the policy of free Jewish immigration, implementing the "Law of the Return," there must be a coordinated flow of capital for investment—and not limited merely to refugee capital that so frequently in the past has had to face discrimination and confiscation. The "Law of the Return" of Jewish immigrants and the flow of refugee and investment capital are twin brothers under the skin. For the sake of the new state of Israel, such a course is indispensable, for only with the influx of refugee capital can we support a progressive program of immigration and colonization.

Yet, even after currency stabilization shall have been achieved and the influx of refugee capital encouraged, the economic survival of Israel will depend largely upon learning the lessons from American experience in the development of a modern economy, based upon large-scale production of needs and services for the common man. At the present time, America also has practically solved the problem of unemployment, even though it may be argued that $40 billion of annual expenditure for defense purposes—representing over 10 per cent of the annual income—may be largely responsible for this highly desirable situation. Where Israel has established cooperative farm settlements to drain off the unemployed, America has used the more radical remedy of the presence of a cold war to bolster its economy. It may be argued that even after it may no longer be necessary to provide such excessive war material, we should still proceed as if it were incumbent upon us to incur similar large expenditures— as if a cold war were yet in existence. Better still, it may well be desirable to continue the expenditures of large sums for public improvements (as already envisaged in a huge national road program) as a moral and financial equivalent of war.

Indeed, public works and cooperative farm settlements, even when both have to be nationally subsidized, must be considered as great war measures—war against poverty and unemployment. So well has Israel already learned this valuable lesson by instituting such a system of cooperative farm settlements, in addition to its necessarily large preparations for defense, that America may well profit from its example: this unique use of farm labor colonies in draining off the possible surplus unemployed, whenever national defense no longer requires an exaggerated and often unbalanced budget.

America, in addition to serving as an example of a free economy based upon a stabilized currency, has also rendered exceptional technological aid to the infant state of Israel. The most conspicuous example of this is the contribution of Professor Walter Clay Lowdermilk, the outstanding soil conservation expert, who spent over two years in Israel as a representative of the United Nations Food and Agricultural Organization. His conclusion is a matter of worldwide significance:

"Israel, while working in its own interest, is becoming a pilot area in building both on misused and erosion-wasted lands a demonstration of how a people may reverse the long decline that has blighted the cradle of western civilization from the Garden of Eden until today. Restoration of these old lands is necessary in the full redemption of the land by Israel. But in doing so, the people of Israel are showing the way to poverty-stricken and under-developed parts of the world that now comprise fully one billion five hundred million people, how to earn some of the good things of life, too. These areas now are a seed bed of social unrest and violent revolution that endangers the peace of the world. The Jewish settlements furnish a pattern for the release of the energies and capacities of so great a number of the world's population. These settlements may well be studied to this end."

Highly significant is the impression that the state of

121

Israel has made upon the new states, harboring many millions of the colored race in Asia and Africa, who are continually sending their representatives to Israel to study these advanced forms of social organization and to learn the new methods of modern economy.

It is, therefore, not the mere emergence of Israel as a state that is so significant, but rather the development from such a state of institutions which together may fittingly be described as a social commonwealth, based upon public corporations established for the benefit of consumers, and fortified by cooperative farm settlements—a system of coexistence with private industry, in which both public and private corporations will compete for the benefit of the body public as a whole.

Objection has sometimes been taken by peace-loving people to the methods employed in the organization of the state of Israel and the necessity of utilizing war as an essential factor in its establishment. But the war of Israel independence was unmistakably a war of self-defense— much more even than the American Revolution—for it was a question of sheer Jewish survival against the Arab hordes concentrating literally on all four borders of the incipient state, with only the waters of the Mediterranean to receive the remnant of survivors in case of defeat. The people of Israel had in fact and not in mere rhetorical phraseology the choice of "liberty or death."

Besides, in the larger synthesis of world values, was it not more important to preserve for future development the survivors of those Children of Israel who developed the Hebrew Bible rather than to permit western Palestine to revert to the Arab desert of the last one thousand years? More especially, when little Palestine composed less than 2 per cent of the vast domains allotted to the Arabs? This was no question of colonial conquest for the benefit of some distant rulers, as in the case of British India.

True, there was here a classic example of a Jewish minority converting itself into a majority, perhaps against the will of the Arab population, although even that is questionable, since external pressure from the Arab states made a possible adjustment with the local Arab population impracticable. But at its worst the Arab-Jewish conflict over Palestine was a struggle to free the derelict land of Israel and save it for civilization.

I know that America has sometimes been criticized for taking Texas and California in the Mexican War—as an act of aggression. But I question the value of this criticism when the alternative would have been to deprive the whole Southwest of the benefits of American civilization. Where there is virtually an empty territory, the world cries for its redemption, and depopulated Palestine was a miniature Texas. The logic of history requires that empty spaces be filled, for nature does "abhor a vacuum," and neither the early pioneer Yankee settlers of Texas, nor the later Chalutzim from the Russian-Jewish pale of settlement, could be prevented from redeeming the soil.

There is a world of difference between "colonies," the *bête noir* of the new Asian-African bloc of nations, and "colonization," the time-honored principle of conquest by settlement, of which America is the classic example.

Indeed, as we progress in culture, we often become squeamish in our judgment of our forefather pioneers. Thus Great Britain, reverting from its policies of colonialism, now pays tribute for its life-saving oil to a few petty sheiks who rule almost empty spaces along the Arabian desert. But there is a world of difference between attempting to dominate a vast colonial empire like India,

123

and occupying a small oil sheikdom along the Persian Gulf. In the latter case, England would have done far better for itself and for the world at large if she would have colonized these oil-rich territories with her own people—as she occupied Australia and New Zealand—now that air-conditioning makes it possible for people of the temperate zone to live and thrive in the tropics.

In the first half century of the modern Jewish colonization of Palestine, peace and the good will of the native Arab population was largely preserved, and every acre of land obtained by Jewish settlers was paid at its greatly inflated value. It was only after the Arab riots started, as a prelude to World War II, that racial strife was engendered and evolved to such an extent as to interfere with Jewish colonization efforts. In the whole history of seventy years before the establishment of the state of Israel, in 1948, the Jewish pioneers followed the precepts of the Quakers in settling Pennsylvania, safeguarding the rights of the indigenous population. And yet even the settlers in Pennsylvania later had to defend themselves against attack of the natives. But in the larger perspective of history who can doubt that William Penn was right in carving out Penn's Woods, as a proper home for European civilization. That is precisely what the Jewish pioneers in Palestine have accomplished in their heartbreaking efforts extending over two generations by redeeming the fringe of Western Asia which had virtually remained a manmade desert for a millennium and a half. And now that the state of Israel is firmly established, the equal rights of all the inhabitants on the principle of "consent of the governed" is safeguarded for the Arab minority, the various Christian groups, as well as for the Jewish majority.

The truth is that England took a long time to learn the

lesson from the American Revolution, with its doctrine of ruling by the "consent of the governed." She belatedly accepted that principle in Canada, half a century after American independence, and so saved that valuable dominion for the British Commonwealth. But then Canada represented a sector of her own people and even the French Canadians could be absorbed as an allied race. Even then Great Britain could not bring herself to incorporate this vast territory of Canada into a real federal union, perhaps because at that time there was neither the telegraph nor efficient steamship navigation to bind together the parts of the empire.

The Northwest Ordinance of 1787, in the newly freed United States, set an example which most nations could not follow at that time because, unlike America, they were not based upon the principle of the "consent of the governed." At that early date, America took the momentous step, even before the Federal Union was formally established, in recognizing the portion of the territory beyond the Alleghenies as equally entitled to form states on the same basis as the thirteen original states. From this has come the five great midwestern states of Ohio, Indiana, Michigan, Illinois and Wisconsin. That was a great act of statemanship, for it freed America from the incubus of colonialism and assured that the "consent of the governed" was a fundamental principle in American democracy.

But the manifest destiny of the newly formed Federal Union saw no inconsistency in the practice of occupying the adjacent territories of Spain, France and Mexico— perhaps just because the door remained open for equal participation of the native population in the formation of new states. Had Great Britain applied the same principle of government, her ever-growing population would have

125

spread beyond Canada and Australasia to the small but strategic outposts of Gibraltar, Aden and the rich oil districts of Arabia. This may be denominated "conquest by settlement," wherein Israel borrows the American principle, but it is free from the taint of colonialism or the attempted rule over natives by "superior races." It was the misfortune of Great Britain that she retained for too long that theme of superiority over native races which is exemplified in Kipling's phrase of "lesser breeds without the law."

Little Israel, by following the American principle of incorporating her "native" population as equals (for despite partisan disputes over treatment of the indigenous Arab population, they are rapidly becoming absorbed as part of the Israeli community), has become a shining light in the East, and is pointing the right path to follow: away from colonialism and forward to the goal of equal rights, for nations as well as for individuals, for states as well as for minority groups.

Reviewing the fateful years which began with the Declaration of Independence of the state of Israel on May 14, 1948, we may be well prepared to compare this decade with the epochal days in the biblical stories of the Exodus from Egypt. Indeed, the miraculous crossing of the withered arm (Yom Suf) in the resurgent waters of the Red Sea, may appear no more wonderful than the departure from Palestine of the British military forces and the flight of the main body of Arabs that followed in its wake. Future historians may regard this reversed exodus as equally remarkable, and theologians in the days to come may point to the "Finger of God" which made it possible for the land of Israel, within a decade of its independence, to absorb more than one million displaced persons, rescued from the European catastrophe of World War II, and the refugees from Moslem lands, which doubled its population. The independence day of the state of Israel has already been proclaimed as a Jewish holiday, exactly two weeks after Passover—the first and only additional day of rest in the Jewish calendar in over two thousand years.

If a restored Israel is symbolic of the new Atomic Age, with which it is intimately associated, it likewise points to a new era in which social justice for all people must take the place of policies of imperialism and domination of "native races." It is in such a message for humanity at large that the great experiment in cooperative settlement likewise means so much. "Zion shall be redeemed with Justice" is more than a mere prophetical phrase in Jewish history. This represents a striving, often unconscious, in the minds of great leaders of social reform in the modern age, even as the prophets and poets of the past proclaimed that message so loudly from the hills of Galilee and the mountains of Judea.

It was not a mere coincidence that the United States, through President Truman, was the first to recognize the infant state of Israel on the very afternoon that the state declared its independence in May, 1948. From Washington's famous letter to the Hebrew congregation at Newport, Rhode Island, and the deep interest that President John Adams evinced for the revival of the Hebrew state down through the days when President Wilson so earnestly threw his support to Great Britain in endorsing the Balfour Declaration for a Jewish homeland in Palestine, the American people have consistently supported the ideal of a Jewish commonwealth. This is best evidenced in the unanimous vote of the Congress of the United States, in 1922, supporting the grant of a Palestine mandate for the establishment of a Jewish homeland. That support, accordingly, was not limited merely to the generous contributions of American Jews during the last generation, involving literally many hundreds of millions of dollars, but also the declarations of support from leaders in public life, irrespective of religious or political affiliation. Indeed, from the early colonial days, and later when the Constitution of the United States was being formed, there was outspoken comparison with biblical history and the ideals of the ancient Israel commonwealth.

Such a commonwealth of Israel may afford the opportunity for practical realization of the great social dreams of the prophets of Israel. This historic reunion of the Jews with their ancestral soil bids well to bring us a new chapter to add to the Bible of old—not yet formulated in words, but already being slowly enacted in deeds by the pioneers from the Emek of Galilee down to the wastes of the Negev, including the vale of Sharon, and up to the mountain of Zion.

During the last 1888 years, since the destruction of the Second Temple by the Romans, the Jews as a people have had the privilege only of denouncing injustice, but never the opportunity of playing a positive role in social statesmanship. Once the Hebraic spirit of social justice—so evident both in the biblical period of Jewish history and in the days of the Maccabean Revival—is permitted the full expression of its genius in social legislation, we may expect a new message from Zion of worldwide significance. Israel, restored once more to its Homeland, will pick up again the thread of its history and continue its allotted task in striving for social justice among men and nations.

128

Date Due

FE 21 '63	MAR 3 1 '75		
MR 8 '63	APR 2 1 '75		
JA 31 '65			
JY 6 '65	MAY 1 '75		
MY 18 '66			
JY 1 '66	MAY 1 8 '75		
MAY 1 '68	E		
NOV 23 '69	NOV 1 1 '88		
MAY 5 '70	NOV 2 '88		
MAY 1 2 '70			
JUN 2 4 '70			
MAY 1 '72			
MAY 8 '74			
E P			
JAN 6 '75			
	PRINTED	IN U. S. A.